Griffoun Society's
Classification System
for
Small Libraries

Developed by

Odette Lapahie

ARCHER TRENT, PUBLISHER

ARCHER TRENT, PUBLISHER
Houston, Texas

GRIFFOUN SOCIETY
Houston, Texas
1 (281) 409-4517
GriffounSociety@ProtonMail.com

INTRODUCTION & INSTRUCTIONS

The *Dewey Decimal System*, I am the first to admit, is a work of sheer genius. But it is not very suitable for small libraries of the humanities. It is much too specific. Many classification numbers under the *Dewey System* are ridiculously long. Even figuring out how some works should be classified under the *Dewey System* is enough to give any librarian not professionally trained a splitting headache (if not a complete nervous breakdown).

Other systems, such as the *Library of Congress System*, share the same disadvantages for small libraries of the humanities managed by amateur librarians.

This *Griffoun Society Classification System for Small Libraries* is designed for libraries of the humanities--not technical libraries of any sort--consisting of no more than a few thousand volumes. Every work can be classified with one to four letters. Numerals are not used. A basic outline immediately follows this Introduction & Instructions.

In case you have never before set about to classify a library, let me offer a few suggestions or pointers that might make the job somewhat less stressful:

- **First,** always use the most specific classification justifiable.
- **Second,** when trying to decide between two or more possible classifications, ask yourself for whom the work was created and who will be its most-likely reader. For example, a book on courtship and marriage might be classified under Home Arts of under Sociology, depending on the considerations already mentioned. And books on sailing might be classified under aquatic sports or under maritime transportation.
- **Third,** don't agonize overmuch about assigning the perfect classification to every single difficult-to-classify book. Remember that classification is primarily for the benefit of casual browsers. Serious researchers that know what they are interested in will rely on the library's catalog, which might take the form of an old-fashioned card catalog or a data base.
- **Fourth,** whenever you are having difficulty deciding how to classify any work, make use of the Index, which follows the Schedules in this volume.
- **And finally,** within each classification, books are traditionally arranged alphabetically by the author's surname. There are a few exceptions. Some books cite no author. In such cases, order by editor if one is named or by publisher otherwise. Motion pictures should be alphabetized by title. A reminder to that effect appears next to the classification in the schedules. To facilitate the process of placing books on shelves in proper order, the first three letters of the author's name (or editor's name, publisher's name, or movie title) should appear directly below the classification. The spine tag for this book, *Griffoun Society's Classification System for Small Libraries*, should look like this:

CAI
LAP

If you still have questions regarding the use of this classification system or relating in any way to organizing your own library, feel free to reach out to me at the Griffoun Society Library. I always find it extremely gratifying to be able to feel that I have helped someone (anyone). I believe other members of the Griffoun Society feel the same way. So don't be shy. We'd love to hear from you.

Odette Lapahie

Basic Outline

A   General Works

B   Beliefs & Values of Humanity (Religion, Philosophy, & Superstition)

C   Information Storage & Retrieval (including Computer Science & Library Science)

D   Language Arts & Communication

E   The Arts in General

F   Works of Fiction by Individual Authors

G   Literature
- GPD   Book Stores & Bookselling
- GR   Poetry

H   Dramatic Arts

I   Visual Art
- INJ   Photography

J   Music
- JV   Dance

K   Recreation

L   Home Arts

M   Applied Arts (Crafts & Traces, including Architecture & Construction, Woodworking, Ceramics, Glass Craft, Furniture, Upholstery, & Metal Craft)

N   Science
- NN   Natural History

O   Applied Science (Technoogy, Engineering, & Manufacturing)

P   Social Sciences
- PA   Education
- PB   Economics
- PC   Business Arts
- PD   Political Science
- PE   Law
- PF   Police Science (including Private Security, Self-Defense, & Martial Arts)
- PG   Criminal Justice, Penology, Corrections, & Rehabilitation
- PH   Military Science
- PI   Naval Science

Q   Behavioral Sciences
- QA   Cultural Anthropology
- QB   Sociology
- QC   General Psychology

R   Health Sciences
- RRI   Psychiatry & Clinical Psychology

S   Nature's Bounty (including Foraging, Conservation, Prospecting, & Mining)

T   Agricultural Science

U   Veterinary Science

V   History

W   Geography, Cartography, Maps, & Travel

X   Transportation

SCHEDULES

A	**General Works** (including General Collected Monographs)
AA	Encyclopedias of General Knowledge
AB	Yearbooks of a General Knowledge
AC	Periodicals of a General Nature
AD	Mysteries
AE	Associations, Fraternal Orders, & Secret Societies
AF	Superlatives
	EXAMPLE: *Guinness Book of World Records*
AG	Curiosities & Oddities (including Collections & Museums of Curiosities & Oddities)
	EXAMPLE: *Ripley's Believe It or Not*

B	**Beliefs & Values of Humanity** (including Religion & Philosophy)
BA	Superstitions, Unfounded Theories, & Patently False Beliefs
BB	**Religion**
	NOTE: Class Comparative Religion here.
BC	Paganism, Tribal Religions, & Ancient & Prehistoric Systems of Belief (including Druidism, Obeah, & Voodoo)
BCA	Mythology & Oral Traditions
BD	**Judaism**
BDA	Hebrew Scriptures & Commentaries
BDB	Historical Judaism
BDC	Jewish Sects
BDD	Modern Rabbinical System
BE	**Christianity**
	NOTE: Class Christian Apologetic & Polemics against Christianity here.
BEA	*Holy Bible* & Commentaries
BEB	Historical Christianity
BEBA	Jesus & the Holy Family
BEBB	Saints & Apostles
BEBC	Early Church
BEBD	Reformation
BEBC	Counter-reformation
BEC	Christian Sects, Denominations, & Congregations
BECA	Coptic Christianity
BECB	Eastern Orthodoxy
BECC	Roman Catholicism
BECD	Papacy
BECE	Protestant Denominations
BECF	Latter Day Saints
BF	**Islam**
BFA	*Holy Quran* & Commentaries
BFB	Historic Islam (including the Prophet Muhammad)
BFC	Islamic Sects & Movements
BG	**Oriental Religion & Philosophy**
BGA	Shintoism
BGB	Hinduism
BGC	Buddhism
BGD	Taoism
BGDA	*Tao Te Ching* & Commentaries
BGE	Confucianism
BGEA	*Analects of Confucius* & Commentaries
BH	**Other Religions of South Asia & of the Near & Far East**
BHA	Druze Faith
BHB	Manichaeism

BHC	Zoroastrianism
BHD	Jainism
BHE	Bahá'í Faith
BHF	Sikhism
BI	**Minor Sects, Cults, & New Religions** (including Rastafarians, Aleph or Aum Shinrikyo, Raëlism, Scientology, & the Unification Church)
BJ	**Natural Religion** (including Deists, Freethinkers, Positivists, & Non-theistic & Labour Churches)
BK	**Theology** (including Deities, Angels, Holiness, Heaven, Hell, Demonology, Purgatory, Judgment, Sin, Salvation, Damnation, & Reincarnation)
BL	**Pastoral Counseling** (or Pastoral Theology)
BM	**Ecclesiology** (including Church Organization, Administration, & Finance; also, Religious Symbols, Clerical Hierarchy, & Vestments)
BN	**Worship & Celebration of Life**
BNA	**Rites, Rituals, & Sacraments**
BNB	**Prayer & Benediction**
BNC	**Other Practices & Disciplines Associated with Various Systems of Belief** (including Meditation, Yoga, Self-Flagellation, & Asceticism)

NOTE: Class Meditation & Yoga as a Psychological Self-Help Practice at RRIC. Class Yoga as Self-Help to Physical Health & Well-being at RO. Class Snake-Handling & Faith-Healing at BR.

BO	**The Use of Hymns in Worship**
BP	**Homiletic**
BQ	**Comprehensive & Comparative Works on Holy Writ**
BR	**Faith** (including Faith-Healing & Snake-Handing)
BS	**Revelation & Prophesy** (also, Fortunetelling, Palmistry, Scrying, Ophiomancy, etc)
BT	**Thaumaturgy & Thaumatology** (including Holy Miracles, Magic, Sorcery, & Witchcraft)
BU	**Spiritualism** (including Seances, Apparitions, Spirits, Ghosts, Revenants, & Hauntings)
BV	**Other Magical Creatures & Beings that Figure in Various Belief Systems** (including Zombies, Vampires, Werewolves, Gryphons, Unicorns, Fairies, Gnomes, Elves, Nymphs, & Mermaids)

NOTE: Class Deities, Angels, & Demons at BK.

BW	**Comprehensive Works on Occult Arts & Arcane Knowledge**
BX	**Wisdom, Enlightenment, & Inspiration**

NOTE: Class Personal Philosophies of Life here. This classification is to Philosophy what Natural History is to Earth Science.

BY	**Philosophy** (including Comparative Philosophy & History of Philosophy)
BYA	**Classical Philosophy**
BYB	**Medieval Philosophy**
BYC	**Modern Philosophy**
BYCA	**Rationalism, Materialism, Humanism, & Existentialism**
BYD	**Logic**
BYE	**Metaphysics** (Structure of Reality)

BYF	**Philosophical Cosmology** (Nature of the Universe)
BYFA	**Ontology** (Nature of Existence)
BYG	**Epistemology** (Possibility & Limits of Knowledge)
BYH	**Axiology** (Nature of Value & Valuation)
BYI	**Ethics** (Moral Philosophy, including Virtue & Vice)
	NOTE: Class Free Will here; also, Determinism.
BYJ	**Aesthetics** (Philosophy of Beauty)
BYK	**Political & Social Philosophy**

C   **Information Science** (including Information Storage & Retrieval)

CA	**Library Science**
CAA	Professional Associations of Librarians
CAB	Periodicals & Yearbooks devoted to Library Science
CAC	Matters of Practical, Ethical, or Legal Concern to Librarians
	NOTE: Class Friends of the Library here.
CAD	Study & Teaching of Library Science (including Fellowships, Scholarships, & Schools)
CAE	Historical & Geographical Treatment of Library Science (including Great Libraries of the Past)
CAF	Library Supplies, Equipment, & Furniture
CAG	Library Management & Record-keeping
CAH	Maintaining & Updating the Collection (including Acquisitions & Book Repairs)
CAHA	Special Collections
CAI	Classification & Organization
CAJ	Cataloging
CAK	Library Users & User Services
CAKA	Library Research & Research Assistance
CB	Microfilm & Microfiche Records

CC	**Computer Science**
	NOTE: Class Computer Engineering at OIH, Computer Manufacturing at OJF, & Internet at DR.
CCA	Computer Hardware (including Peripheral Devices)
	NOTE: Class Computer Engineering at OIH.
CCB	Software & Applications
CCBA	Coding & Software Development
CCBB	Operating Systems
CCBC	Artificial Intelligence
CCC	Computerized Information Storage & Retrieval (including Floppy Discs, Tape, Cloud Storage, External Hard Drives, Flash Drives, SD Cards, etc)
CD	Information Storage via Audio & Video Recording

D	**Language Arts & Communication**
DA	Dictionaries & Thesauruses
DAA	Polyglot Dictionaries
DB	Associations Devoted to Language Arts & Communication
DC	Periodicals & Yearbooks Devoted to Language Arts & Communication
DD	Study & Teaching of Language Arts & Communications (including Fellowships, Scholarships, & Schools) NOTE: Class Grammarr & Usage here.
DDA	Study & Teaching of English as a Foreign Language (or ESL)
DDB	Study & Teaching of Foreign Languages
DE	Translation
DF	Etymology
DG	Written Language (including Penmanship & Calligraphy, Phonetics, Orthography, Standard Abbriviations, & Punctuation) NOTE: Class Creative Writing or Composition at GPA
DGA	Reading for Comprehension NOTE: Class Reading for Pleasure & Edification at GE.
DH	Signs, Sign-Lettering, & Related Arts NOTE: Class Stone-Engraving & Neon Signs here.
DI	Speech (including Diction, Pronunciation, & Oratory or Public Speaking)
DJ	Communication through Symbols (including Language of Flowers & of Gems)
DK	Body Language & Facial Expressions
DL	Signing & Sign Languages
DM	Semaphore Communication
DN	**Cryptology & Cryptography**
DO	Telegraphy & Teleprinter Communication
DP	Telephony
DQ	Wireless Communication NOTE: Class Radio Communication here.
DR	Internet, eMail, Texting, SMS, & Social Media

E   **The Arts in General** (including Comprehensive Works on the Arts & Humanities.Dictionaries & Encyclopedias of the Arts in General, Associations Devoted to the Arts, & Periodicals & Yearbooks Devoted to the Arts)

EA   **Study & Teaching of the Arts in General** (including Appreciation & Enjoyment of the Arts)

EB   **Historical & Geographical Treatment of the Arts** (including History of Arts Communities, Biographies of Individuals (such as Jean Cocteau & Alexander King) Associated with Multiple Areas of the Arts)

F   **Works of Fiction** (including Collected Works of Fiction by Individual Authors & Critiques & Synopses of Individual Works of Fiction)
NOTE: Alphabetize critiques & synopses not by the authors of those critiques & synopses but by the authors of the works of fiction being written about.
NOTE: Class Anthologies of Fiction by Multiple Authors under G.

G	Literature
GA	Dictionaries & Encyclopedias Related to Literature
GB	Associations Devoted to Literature & its Creation, Appreciation, & Enjoyment
GC	Literary Journals & Yearbooks
GD	Study & Teaching of Literature (including Fellowships & Scholarships, Schools, Tutorials, & Museums)
GE	Appreciation & Enjoyment of Literature (including Reading for Pleasure & Edification; also, Literary Theory)
GF	Literary Prizes & Awards
GG	**History of Literature** (including Collected Literary Works, Criticisms, & Biographies & Diaries of Authors)
GGA	Folk Literature
GGB	Ancient Literature of the World
GGC	Medieval Literature of the World
GGD	Renaissance Literature of the World
GGE	Literature of the 18th Century of the World
GGF	Literature of the 19th Century of the World
GGG	Literature of the 20th Century of the World
GGH	Literature of the 21st Century of the World
GH	**English-Language Literature**
GHB	Medieval English-Language Literature
GHC	Renaissance English-Language Literature
GHD	English-Language Literature of the 18th Century
GHE	English-Language Literature of the 19th Century
GHF	English-Language Literature of the 20th Century
GHG	English-Language Literature of the 21st Century
GI	French Literature
GJ	German Literature
GK	Russian Literature
GL	Spanish-Language Literature
GM	Literature of Other Languages
GN	**Literature for, by, or about Specific Groups**
GNA	Women
GNB	Blacks
GNC	Hispanics
GND	Indigenes
GNE	Other Groups
GO	**Literary Themes**
GOA	Juvenile Literature (Literature for Juvenile Readers)
GOB	Non-Fiction (Comprehensive Works)
GOC	Literary Fiction (including So-Called Novels of Manners)
GOD	Literary Humor
GOE	Erotic Literature & Romantic Love Stories
GOF	Detective & Crime Stories (including Thrillers, Spy Novels, & Intrigues)

GOG	Historical & Period Fiction
GOGA	Western Adventures
GOH	Fantasy
GOHA	Science Fiction
GOI	Horror
GOJ	Graphic Novels & Comic Strips

GP   **Books & the Printed Word**
NOTE: Class Reading for Edification & Pleasure at GE.

GPA	Composition & Creative Writing (including Copyright Protection & Plagiarism)
GPB	Editing, Proofreading, & Publishing (including Publishing of Periodicals, Audio Books, & Podcasts)
GPC	Bindery
GPD	Bookstores & Bookselling

GQ   **Journalism**
NOTE: Class Newspaper & Magazine Publishing at GPB. Class Photojournalism at INJP.

GR   **Poetry**

GRA	Dictionaries & Encyclopedias Related to Poetry
GRB	Associations Devoted to Poetry, its Creation, Appreciation, & Enjoyment
GRC	Periodicals & Yearbooks Devoted to Poetry
GRD	Study & Teaching of Poetry (including Fellowships & Scholarships, Schools, Tutorials, & Museums)
GRE	Poesy & Poetics (including Appreciation & Enjoyment of Poetry & Writing Poetry)
GREA	Narrative Verse (including Epic Poetry & Ballads)
GREB	Pastoral Verse
GREC	Lyrical Poetry (including Ekphrases, Odes, & Elegies)
GRED	Love Poems & Erotic Verse
GREE	Sonnets
GREF	Light Verse (including Limericks, Clerihews, Palindromes, Acrostics, & Golden Shovels)
GREG	Blank Verse
GREH	Juvenile Verse
GREI	Other Forms of Poetry (Haiku, Dizain, Sestina, Rondel, Villanelle, Ghazal, Triolet, Cinquain, Paradelle, etc)
GRF	Poetry Prizes & Awards
GRG	History of Poetry (including Collected Poetic Works, Criticisms, & Biographies of Poets)
GRGA	Poetry of the Ancient World
GRGB	Medieval Poetry of the World
GRGC	World Poetry of the Renaissance Period
GRGD	World Poetry of the 18th Century
GRGE	World Poetry of the 19th Century

GRGF	World Poetry of the 20[h] Century
GPGG	World Poetry of the 21st Century
GRH	**English-Language Poetry** (including British, American, Australian, etc)
GRHB	Medieval English Poetry
GRHC	Renaissance English Poetry
GRHD	English Poetry of the 18th Century
GRHE	English Poetry of the 19th Century
GRHF	English Poetry of the 20th Century
GRHG	English Poetry of the 21st Century
GRI	French Poetry
GRJ	German Poetry
GRK	Russian Poetry
GRL	Spanish-Language Poetry
GRM	Poetry of Other Languages
GRN	**Poetry for, by, or about Specific Groups**
GRNA	Women
GRNB	Blacks
GRNC	Hispanics
GRND	Indigenes
GRNE	Other Groups

H	Dramatic Arts
HA	Dictionaries & Encyclopedias Devoted to Dramatic Arts
HB	Associations Devoted to Dramatic Arts
HC	Periodicals & Yearbooks Devoted to Dramatic Arts
HD	Matters of Practical, Ethical, or Legal Concern to Persons Working in Fields Related to Dramatic Arts (including Theatrical Awards)
HE	Related Arts & Science to Dramatic Arts
HF	Study & Teaching of Dramatic Arts (including Fellowships & Scholarships, Acting Schools, & Tutorials)
HG	Geographical & Historical Treatment of Dramatic Arts
HI	Theory & Philosophy of Dramatic Arts
HJ	Appreciation & Enjoyment of Dramatic Arts
HK	**Writing Plays**
HL	Stage Production
HM	Acting
HN	Directing
HO	Stage Lighting
HP	Set Design
HQ	Theatrical Props & Costumes
HR	Theaters & Theater Management (also, Promotion of Stage Plays, including Playbills & Posters for Stage Plays)
HS	Types of Dramatic Works
HSA	Tragedy
HSB	Comedy
HSC	Tragicomedy
HSD	Melodrama
HSE	Musical Drama
HSF	Other Types of Dramatic Works (including Absurdist, Political, & Historical Drama; also, Morality Plays)
HT	**Dramatic Works** (including Play Scripts, Synopses, Reviews, Production Notes, & Recordings of Actual Productions)

NOTE: Arrange alphabetically by playwright' surname.

NOTE: Some libraries might choose to put media other than books in an entirely different location, but that media, such as CDs & DVDs, will still need to be classified. The Griffoun Society Library, for which this system was developed, has such a scant few DVDs & CDS that it elects to place them on the same shelves with books.

HU	**Broadcast Entertainment** (including Radio & Television Drama & Comprehensive Works on the Broadcast Industry)
HV	**Motion-Picture Arts & Sciences**
HVA	Dictionaries & Encyclopedias Related to Motion Pictures
HVB	Associations Devoted to Motion Pictures (including Fan Clubs)

HVC	Periodicals & Yearbooks Devoted to Motion Pictures
HVD	Matters of Practical, Ethical, or Legal Concern to Persons Working in Fields Related to Motion Pictures (including Awards, Censorship, & Rating Systems)
HVE	Related Arts & Science to Motion Pictures
HVF	Study & Teaching of Motion Picture Arts & Sciences (including Fellowships & Scholarships, Film Schools, Tutorials, & Movie Museums)
HVG	Geographical & Historical Treatment of Motion-Picture Entertainment
	NOTE: Class Biographies of Actors, Producers, & Directors here.
HVH	Theory & Philosophy of Motion-Picture Entertainment
HVI	Equipment, Tools, & Supplies Related to Motion-Picture Production & Exhibition
HVJ	Appreciation & Enjoyment of Motion Pictures
HVK	Script Writing & Adaptation
HVL	Motion-Picture Production
HVM	Screen Acting
HVN	Motion-Picture Directing
HVO	Motion-Picture Lighting
HVP	Motion-Picture Set Design
HVQ	Motion-Picture Props & Costumes
HVR	Cinematography
HVS	Film & Digital Editing & Post-Production
HVT	Release & Exhibition
	NOTE: Class Motion-Picture Theaters here.
HVU	Motion-Picture Promotion (including Movie Posters & Trailers)
	NOTE: Class individual Trailers by movie title at KVY. Class Collected Trailers here.
HVV	Motion-Picture Stunts & Special Effects
HVW	Animation
HVX	Types of Motion Pictures
HVXA	Short Films
HVXB	Documentaries & Instructional Films
HVXC	Docudramas
HVXD	Westerns
HVXE	Horror Films
HVXF	Comedies & Rom-Coms
HVXG	Musicals
HVXH	Other

HVY   **Motion Pictures** (including Scripts, Synopses, Reviews, Trailers, DVDs of Movies, etc)

Note: Arrange alphabetically by title.

NOTE: Some libraries might choose to put media other than books in an entirely different section of the library, but those media, such as CDs & DVDs, will still need to be classified. The Griffoun Society Library, for which this system was developed, has such a scant few DVDs & CDs that it elects to place them on the same shelves with books.

HV   **Pageantry** (including Parades)
HW   Mimes, Clowns, Jugglers, & Circuses
HX   Burlesque Theatre (including Vaudeville, Stand-up Comedy, & Strip Tease)

I	Visual Art
	NOTE: Class Fine Art here.
IA	Dictionaries & Encyclopedias Devoted to Visual Art
IB	Associations Devoted to Visual Art
IC	Periodicals & Yearbooks Devoted to Visual Art
ID	Matters of Practical, Ethical, or Legal Concern to Persons Working in Fields Related to Visual Art
IE	Related Arts & Science to Visual Art (including Anatomy for the Artist)
IF	Study & Teaching of Visual Art (including Fellowships & Scholarships, Art Schools, & Tutorials)
IFA	Art Museography (including Catalogs of Exhibitions)
IFB	Art Museology (including Art Restoration, Preservation, & Framing)
IG	**Geographical & Historical Treatment of Visual Art**
IGA	Prehistoric Art of the World
IGB	Ancient Art of the World
IGC	World Art of the Middle Ages 476 CE – 1453 CE
IGD	World Art of the late Middle Ages 1453 CE – 1700 CE
IGE	18th Century Art of the World
IGF	19th Century Art of the World
IGG	20th Century Art of the World
IGH	21st Century Art of the World
IGI	**European Art & Art of & of the Islands of the Atlantic Ocean**
	(also, Comprehensive works on Art of the Western World)
IGIA	Prehistoric European Art
IGIB	Ancient European Art
IGIC	European Art of the Middle Ages 476 CE – 1453 CE
IGID	European Art of the Renaissance
IGIE	European Art of the 18th Century
IGIF	European Art of the 19th Century
IGIG	European Art of the 20th Century
IGIH	European Art of the 21st Century
IGJ	African Art
IGK	Middle Eastern & South Asian Art & Art of Indian Ocean Islands
IGL	Far Eastern Art (including Art of Southeast Asia & Malaysia)
IGM	Art of Australia, New Zealand, & the Pacific Islands
IGN	Art of the Western Hemisphere & Caribbean Sea
IGO	**North American Art** (including Central American Art)
IGOA	Pre-Columbian Art
IGOB	North American Art 1492 CE – 1700 CE
IGOC	North American Art of the 18th Century
IGOD	North American Art of the 19th Century
IGOE	North American Art of the 20th Century
IGOF	North American Art of the 21st Century
IGP	South American Art

IGQ	**Visual Art for, by, or about Specific Groups** (including Comprehensive Works on Artists Belonging to Specific Groups)	
IGQA	Women	
IGQB	Blacks	
IGQC	Hispanics	
IGQD	Indigenes	
IGQE	Other Groups	
IH	**Theory & Philosophy of Art** (also, Buying & Collecting Art, Art Appreciation & Criticism)	
II	Art Supplies (including Clip Art)	
IJ	**Studio Art**	
IJA	Perspective	
IJB	Composition	
IJC	Line & Color	
IJD	Design	
IJE	Commercial Art	
IJF	Symbolism in Art	
IJG	Individual Artistic Style	
IJH	Creating Art with Artificial Intelligence	
IK	**Themes in Art**	
IKA	Iconographic Art	
IKB	Religious Art	
IKC	Human Figure (including Nude & Erotic Art)	
IKD	Portraits	
IKDA	Animal Portraits & Wildlife	
IKE	Genre Art	
IKF	Landscapes, Nature, Seascapes, & Cityscapes	
IKG	Still Life	
IKGA	Vehicles & Machinery	
IKH	Non-objective Art	
IL	**Public Art**	
IM	Primitive or Folk Art (including Artworks by Children)	
IN	**Art Media & Ways of Working in Various Media**	
INA	Painting	
INAA	Oil & Acrylic	
INAB	Alla Prima Painting	
INAC	Plein Air Painting	
INAD	Impasto	
INAE	Watercolor	
INAF	Gouache	
INAG	Encaustic	
INAH	Murals (including Fresco Technique)	
INAI	Other Methods	
INB	Drawing & Sketching (Pencil, Pen-&-Ink, Crayon, Charcoal, & Pastels)	
INC	Illustration, Illumination, & Cartooning	
IND	Printmaking (Etching, Lithography, Serigraphy, Woodcut, Linocut, etc)	

INE	Mosaic
INF	**Sculpture**
ING	Assemblage
INH	Decoupage & Mixed Media (including Collage & Montage)
INI	Other Media & Methods of Working
INJ	**Photography**
INJA	Dictionaries & Encyclopedias of Photography & Related Arts & Sciences
INJB	Associations Devoted to Photography & its Related Arts & Sciences
INJC	Periodicals & Yearbooks Devoted to Photography & Related Arts & Sciences by Title
INJD	Matters of Practical, Ethical, or Legal Concern to Photographers & to Persons in Fields Related to Photography NOTE: Class Photography Contests & Awards here.
INJE	Related Arts & Science to Photography
INJF	Study & Teaching of Photography & of Arts & Sciences Related to Photography (including Fellowships & Scholarships, Schools, Tutorials, & Museums of Photography)
INJG	Appreciating & Collecting Photography as Art (including Photographic Theory)
INJH	**Geographical & Historical Treatment of Photography**
INJI	Photographic Equipment, Supplies, & Services
INJJ	Studio Photography (also, Comprehensive works on Professional Photography, Composition, Lighting, Exposure, Focus, Depth of Field, Pose, & Mood)
INJK	Darkroom & Photofinishing (including Developing & Printing, Retouching, Lightroom®, Photo Manipulation, PhotoShop®, Mounting, & Framing)
INJL	Location Photography (including Night Photography & Available-Light Photography)
INJM	Commercial & Fashion Photography
INJN	Industrial, Medical, & Other Highly Technical Fields
INJO	Event Photography EXAMPLE: Wedding & Bar Mitzvah Photography
INJP	Photojournalism & Sports Photography
INJQ	Themes in Fine-Art Photography (comprehensive works & any theme not specifically mentioned below)
INJR	Portrait Photography (including Casual or Street Portraits & Animal Portraits)
INJS	Erotic & Nude Photography (including Glamour & Pin-up Photography)
INJT	Landscape Photography
INJU	Architectural Photography
INJV	Still-Life Photography
INJW	Amateur Snap-shooting, Photo Montage, & Photo Albums

J	**Music** (also Comprehensive Works on Music & Dance)	
JA	Dictionaries & Encyclopedias Related to Music	
JB	Associations Devoted to Music	
JC	Periodicals & Yearbooks Devoted to Music	
JD	Matters of Practical, Ethical, or Legal Concern to Persons Working in Fields Related to Music (including Music Awards)	

EXAMPLE: Copyright Protection & Infringement; also, Comprehensive Works on the Music Business

JE	Related Arts & Science to Music
JF	Study & Teaching of Music (including Fellowships & Scholarships, Tutorials, & Music Conservatories)
JG	Geographical & Historical Treatment of Music (including Biographies of Musicians & Composers)
JH	Theory & Philosophy of Music (also, Appreciation & Enjoyment of Music)
JI	Musical Instruments & Equipment, Tools, & Supplies Related to Music
JJ	Musical Composition
JJA	Musical Arrangement
JK	**Musical Notation**
JL	Lyrics
JM	Musical Performance
JMA	Concerts & Public Performances
JMB	Voice & Singing
JMC	By Instrument
JMD	Conducting
JME	Recorded Music & the Recording Industry
JN	Program Music
JO	Theatrical Music (including Fanfares, Motion-Picture Themes, & Operatic Music)
JP	**Classical Music**
JQ	Sacred or Ecclesiastical Music
JR	Martial Music
JS	Folk Music
JT	Popular Music
JTA	Ragtime, Blues, Swing, Boogie-Woogie, & Jazz
JTB	Rhythm-&-Blues, Soul, Hip-Hop, & Rap
JTC	Rock-&-Roll
JTD	Country & Western
JTE	New Age
JTF	Other Forms of Popular Music
JU	Sheet Music
JV	**Dance**
JVA	Folk Dancing (including Square Dancing)
JVB	Ballroom Dancing
JVC	Choreography & Dance Notation
JVD	Ballet

| JVE | Modern Dance (including Tap, Jazz, & Break Dance) |
| JVF | Exotic Dance (including Hula & Belly Dance) |

K	Leisure , Relaxation, & Recreation
KA	Dictionaries & Encyclopedias Related to Leisure, Hobbies, Sports, & Recreation
KB	Associations Devoted to Leisure, Hobbies, Sports, & Recreation
KC	Periodicals & Yearbooks Devoted to Leisure, Hobbies, Sports, & Recreation
KD	Matters of Practical, Ethical, or Legal Concern to Persons Working in Sports & in Fields Related to Recreation (Awards, Titles, etc)
KE	Related Arts & Science to Leisure, Hobbies, Sports & Recreation
KF	Study & Teaching of Physical Education, Sports, & Recreation
KG &	Geographical & Historical Treatment of Leisure, Hobbies, Games, Sports, & Recreation (including Sports Statistics & Halls of Fame)
KH	Theory & Philosophy of Leisure, Hobbies, Sports & Recreation (including Competitive versus Non-competitive Sports, Participation versus Spectatorship, & Professional versus Amateur Sports)
KI	Equipment, Supplies, & Facilities for Sports & Recreation
KJ	**Sports & Sporting Events**
KJA	Winter Sports
KJB	Summer Sports
KJC	Team Sports
KJD	Individual Sports
KJE	Track & Field
KJF	Gymnastic
KJG	Equine Sports
KJH	Motor Sports
KJI	Aerial Sports
KJJ	Aquatic & Maritime Sports (including Swimming, Diving, Recreational Boating, & Yatching)
KJK	Combat Sports
KJL	Marksmanship Sports
KJM	Other Sports
KK	Games
KKA	Board Games
KKB	Card Games
KKC	Pinball
KKD	Electronic & Computer Games
KKE	Arcades
KKF	Gaming, Gambling, & Casinos
KL	Puzzles, Riddles, & Brain-Teasers
KM	Jokes, Cartoons, & Humor (including Benefits of Laughter)
	NOTE: Class Stand-up Comedy at HX & Literary Humor at GOD.
KN	Hobbies
KNA	Collecting
KNB	Building & Collecting Models
KNC	Journaling, & Scrapbooking

KO	Wilderness Recreation (including Hiking, Camping, Trophy Hunting, Sports Fishing, & Climbing)
KOA	Wilderness Parks, Picnic Grounds, & Trails
KP	Resorts & Cruise Ships
KQ	Amusement Parks, Theme Parks, Fairs, Carnivals, & Rides
KR	Playgrounds
KS	Toys & Dolls

L	**Home Arts**	
LA	Etiquette	
LB	Grooming & Personal Appearance	

EXAMPLE: *Dress for Success* by John T Molloy

LBA		Cosmetology & Barbering

NOTE: Class Nail Salons here; also, Body Paint & Tattoos.

LBB		Beauty Contests & Titles
LBC		Fashion Models, the Modeling Profession, & Model Agencies

NOTE: Depending upon the focus of a particular library, it might be preferable to classify Artists' Models under IG (Geographical & Historical Treatment of Visual Art).

LBD		Fashions
LC	Wardrobe Maintenance (including Laundry, Ironing, & Dry Cleaning)	
LD	**Friendship & Sexual, Romantic, & Domestic Relationships**	

EXAMPLE: *The Joy of Sex* by Dr Alex Comfort.

NOTE: Class Advice on Marriage, Family Life, & Polyamory Relationships here; also, Guides to Dating & Sexual Pleasure, Masturbation, & Erotic Massage. Class Sociological Studies of Courtship & Marriage Customs at QBQA. Class Sociological Studies of Alternative Forms of Marriage at QBR. Class Physiology of Sex & the Human Reproductive Process at RQA.

LDA		Parenting
LE	Household Finance & Home Economics	
LF	Housekeeping & Dish-washing	
LG	**Hospitality**	
LGA		Party Planning & Entertaining Guests
LGB		Inn-keeping & Hotel Management
LGC		Restaurants & Restaurant Management
LGD		Cookery (including Recipe Books)
LGE		Food & Beverage Service (including Table Settings, Waiting Table, Bartending, & Mixology)
LGEA		Catering
LGF		Dining & Food Appreciation
LGG		Floral Design & Decorating (including Floristry)
LGH		Table Decoration

M   Applied Arts (Crafts & Trades)

MA	**Architecture & Construction**
MAA	Dictionaries & Encyclopedias Related to Architecture & Construction
MAB	Associations Devoted to Architecture & Construction
MAC	Periodicals & Yearbooks Devoted to Architecture & Construction
MAD	Matters of Practical, Ethical, or Legal Concern to Persons Working in Architecture or Construction
	EXAMPLE: Licensing & Regulation
MAE	Related Arts & Science to the Architecture & Construction
	EXAMPLES: Reading Construction Blueprints, Architectural Rendering, & Model-Building for Architects
MAF	Study & Teaching of Architecture & Construction (including Fellowships, Grants, Schools, & Apprenticeships)
MAG	Historical & Geographical Treatment of Architecture & Construction
MAH	Theory & Philosophy of Architecture & Construction
MAI	Construction Tools, Materials, & Supplies
MAJ	**Construction Methods & Materials**
MAJA	Wood Construction (including Framing, Construction Carpentry, & Post-&-Beam Construction)
MAJB	Masonry Construction
MAJC	Adobe Construction
MAJD	Concrete Construction
MAJE	Construction Steel Work
MAJF	Construction Glass Work
MAJG	Earth-sheltered Construction
MAJH	Prefabricated or Modular Construction
	EXAMPLE: Rolling Homes by Jane Lidz
MAJI	Unconventional or Innovative Methods & Materials (including Straw-Bale, Wattle, & Cob Construction)
MAK	**Construction Trades**
MAKA	Construction Electrical Trade
MAKB	Integrated Electronic & Computerized Systems
MAKC	Building Security Systems
MAKD	Heating, Air Conditioning, & Ventilation
MAKE	Plumbing
MAKF	Drywall (including Tape-&-Float)
MKAG	Painting & Finishing
MAKH	Ceilings & Roofs
MAKI	Floors & Stairs
MAKJ	Windows & Doors
MAKK	Cabinetry

MAL	**Renovation, Demolition, Building Maintenance , & Home Improvement**
MAM	Residential Architecture & Construction
MAN	Commercial Architecture & Construction
MAO	Agricultural Architecture & Construction
	EXAMPLES: Barns, Silos, & Stables
MAP	Institutional Architecture & Construction
MAQ	Ecclesiastical Architecture & Construction
MAR	Industrial Architecture & Construction
MAS	**Environmental Architecture**
MASA	Interior Design
MASB	Landscape Architecture (including Parks, Gazebos, Bandstands, Tree Houses, Sheds, Decks, Water Features, & Pathways)
MASC	City Planning
MAT	**Architectural Embellishment**
MB	**Woodcraft**
	NOTE: Class Sawmills at OJM.
MBA	Wood-Carving
	NOTE: Class Netsuke at MM.
MC	Furniture Design & Construction
MCA	Upholstery
MD	**Ceramics, Pottery, Modeling Clay, Papier Mâché, & Acrylic Medium**
ME	Glass Craft
MF	Horology & Chronometry (including Watch- & Clock-Making, Sundials, & Hourglasses)
MG	Jewelry & Lapidary
MGA	Beads, Beading, & Beadwork
MGB	Enameling (Cloisonne)
MH	**Metalcraft**
MHA	Silversmithing & Goldsmithing
MHB	Blacksmithing
MHC	Gunsmithing & Bladesmithing
MHD	Welding, Brazing, Soldering, & Cutting with a Torch
MHE	Machining
MHF	Sheet-Metal Fabrication
MHG	Tin-Punching & Related Crafts
MI	Basketry
MJ	Candle-making
MK	**Textile Arts**
MKA	Looms & Weaving
	NOTE: Class Industrial Weaving at OJK.

MKB	Sewing
	NOTE: Class Garment Industry at OJL.
MKC	Knitting & Crocheting by Hand
MKD	Cross Stitch & other Decorative Needlepoint
MKDA	Tapestry
ML	**Stone-cutting**
	NOTE: Class Quarrying at SH & Stone-Engraving at DH.
MM	Other Crafts (including Netsuke & Comprehensive Works on Native Crafts)

N	**Pure Science**
NA	Dictionaries & Encyclopedias Related to Science
NB	Associations Devoted to Science
NC	Periodicals & Yearbooks Devoted to Science
ND	Matters of Practical, Ethical, or Legal Concern to Scientists
NE	Related Arts & Science to Science
NF	Study & Teaching of Science (including Fellowships & Scholarships, Schools, & Science Museums)
NG	Geographical & Historical Treatment of Science
NH	Theory & Philosophy of Science
	NOTE: Class Scientific Method here.
NI	Science Laboratories (including Equipment, Tools, & Supplies)
NJ	Popular Science
NK	Comprehensive Works on Formal Science

NL	**Mathematics**
NLA	Numbers, Number Theory, & Number Systems
NLB	Counting & Combinatronics
NLC	Arithmetic Operations
NLCA	Slide Rule, Abacus, Adding Machine, & Calculator
NLD	Algebra
NLE	Geometry
NLF	Trigonometry
NLG	Advanced Mathematics (including but not limited to Discrete Mathematics, Mathematical Logic, Set Theory, Statistics, Calculus, Analysis, Mathematical Modeling, Computational Mathematics, Game Theory, & Experimental Mathematics)

NM	**Comprehensive Works on Natural Science**
	NOTE: Natural Science encompasses Earth Science (Geology, Oceanography, & Meteorology) & Life Science (Biology).

NN	**Natural History**
	NOTE: Natural History is the empirical observation of Nature & is often (but not always) conducted by amateur scientists or hobbyists, rather than by professionals. Class Conservation at SA.

NO	**Comprehensive Works on Earth Science**
NP	Geology
NPA	Historical Geology (Paleogeology)
NPB	Seismology
NPC	Vulcanology
NPD	Mineralogy
NPDA	Gemology
NQ	Oceanography
NR	Meteorology

NRA	Climate
NRB	Weather
NRBA	Weather Prognostication
NRBB	Weather Records

NS   **Biology**

NOTE: Biology is also called *Life Science* & encompasses Paleontology, Microbiology, Botany, & Zoology. Class Definition of Life here; also Theories, such as that of Evolution.

NSA	Classification of All Living Things (including Binomial Nomenclature)
NSB	Paleontology
NSC	**Microbiology**
NSCA	Microscopy
NSD	Fungi
NSE	Protista
NSF	Monera
NSG	**Botany** (Study of Plant Life)
NSGA	Study & Teaching of Botany (including Botanical Gardens)
NSGB	Non-flowering Plants (Mosses & Ferns)
NSGC	Flowering Plants
NSGD	Dendrology (Study of Trees & Shrubs)
NSH	**Zoology** (Study of Animal Life)
NSHA	Study & Teaching of Zoology (including Zoological Parks & Taxidermy)
NSHB	Comprehensive Works on Vertebrates

         NOTE: Vertebrates include Reptiles, Amphibians, Birds, Fish, & Mammals.

NSHC	Herpetology (Study of Reptiles & Amphibians)
MSHD	Ornithology (Study of Birds)
MSHE	Oology (Study of Bird Eggs)
MSHF	Ichthyology (Study of Fish)
MSHG	Mammalogy
MSHH	Physical Anthropology
NSHI	Invertebrates (including Insects, Spiders, Snails, Worms, Bivalves, Octopi, Squid, etc)
NSI	**Ecology** (including Biomes & Ecosystems)

         NOTE: Class Conservation at SA.

NT   **Physics**

NU   **Chemistry**

NUA	Alchemy

NV   **Astronomy**

NVA	Astrology
NVB	Amateur Astronomy (including Astronomy Clubs)
NVC	Telescopes & Observatories (also, Radio Astronomy)

NVD	Constellations
NVE	Solar Astronomy (including Seasons of the Year, Sunrise & Sunset, & Calendars)
NVF	Lunar Astronomy
NVG	Planetary Astronomy
NVH	Astrophysics
NVI	Astrochemistry
NVJ	Astrometry, Spectroscopy, Photometry, etc
NVK	Astrogeology
NVL	Astrobiology (including UFOs & Extraterrestrial Life)
NVM	Scientific Cosmology (Evolution of the Universe)

O	**Applied Science** (Technology)
OA	Dictionaries & Encyclopedias Related to Technology, Engineering, & Manufacturing
OB	Associations Devoted to Technology, Engineering, & Manufacturing
OC	Periodicals & Yearbooks Devoted to Technology, Engineering, & Manufacturing
OD	Matters of Practical, Ethical, or Legal Concern to Persons Working in Fields Related to Technology, Engineering, & Manufacturing
	EXAMPLES: Licensing & Regulation
OE	Related Arts & Science to Technology, Engineering, & Manufacturing
OEA	Mechanical Drawing or Drafting
OEB	Computer-Assisted Design
OF	Study & Teaching of Technology, Engineering, & Manufacturing
	(including Fellowships & Scholarships, Schools, Tutorials, & Museums)
OG	Geographical & Historical Treatment of Technology, Engineering, & Manufacturing
	NOTE: Some works on the Industrial Revolution might be classed here.
OH	Theory & Philosophy of Technology, Engineering, & Mass Production
OI	**Engineering**
OIA	Engineering Materials
OIB	Destructive & Non-destructive Testing
OIC	Engineering Management
OID	Mechanical Engineering
OIE	Civil & Structural Engineering
OIF	Sanitation Engineering (including Water Purification & Distribution, Waste Management, & Recycling)
OIG	Electrical & Electronic Engineering
OIH	Computer Engineering
OII	Aerospace Engineering
OIJ	Mechatronics
	NOTE: Mechatronics combines Mechanical Engineering with Electrical & Electronic Engineering, often in Analysis of Automated Systems. Class Guidance Systems, Remote Control, Feedback, Telemetry, Robotics, Cybernetics, Avionics, & Instrumentation here.
OIK	Miniaturization & Nanotechnology
OIL	Acoustical Engineering (Engineering concerned with Analysis & Control of Vibration, particularly of Sound Vibrations)
OIM	Optical Engineering
OIN	Automotive & Vehicular Engineering
OIO	Agricultural Engineering
OIP	Chemical Engineering
OIQ	Petroleum Engineering
OIR	Energy Technology
OIS	Nuclear Engineering
OIT	Industrial Engineering & Factory Design

OIU	Ergonomics
OIV	Efficiency Engineering

OJ	**Manufacturing** (Factory Operation & Production on an Industrial Scale)
OJA	Of Packaged Foods & Nutritional Supplements
OJB	Of Pharmaceutical Products & Toiletries
OJC	Of Toys, Games, & Sports Equipment
OJD	Of Household Goods & Appliances
OJE	Of Lighting Equipment
OJF	Of Consumer & Industrial Electronics
OJG	Of Tools & Machinery
OJH	Of Agricultural Tools, Equipment, & Machinery
OJI	Of Vehicles, Aircraft, & Marine Vessels
OJJ	Of Paints & Chemicals
OJK	Of Textiles (including Industrial Weaving)
OJL	Of Shoes, Hats, Garments, & Fashion Accessories
OJM	Of Construction Materials
	NOTE: Class Sawmills & Lumber Processing here.
OJN	Of Other Products

OK	**Product Packaging**
OL	Other Technologies (including Technologies of the Future)

P   **Social Sciences**

PA   **Education** (includ ng Schools, Teaching, School Administration, Scholarship, & Learning)

PB   **Economics**
              NOTE: Class Environmentalism & Conservation at SA.

PC   **Business Arts** (including Leadership & Management, Entrepreneurship, Negotiation, Rules
              of Order, Office Skills, Business Communications, Human Resources, Financial Management,
              Bookkeeping & Accounting, Asset Management, & Production Management, Distribution,
              Marketing, Advertising & Promotion, & Service Industries)

PD   **Political Science** (including Biographies of Politicians, Types of Government, Branches of
              Government, Levels of Government, Political Parties & Alliances, Lobbyists & Special Interest,
              Elections & Recalls, *Coup d'état*, Citizenship, Civil Rights, Statesmanship, Diplomacy, Standardization
              of Weights & Measure nents, Political Appointments, & Civil Service)
PDA   **Political Movements** (including the Civil Rights Movement, Feminism, & Women's
                   Suffrage Movement)

PE   **Law**

PF   **Police Science** (including Investigation, Patrol, & Undercover Police Operations)
PFA   **Study & Teaching of Police Science** (including Police Academies)
PFB   **History of Law Enforcement**
PFC   **Police Equipment, Weapons, Supplies, Vehicles, Uniforms, &
                   Badges**
PFD   **Neighborhood Watches & Vigilantes**
PFE   **Private Security, Private Investigations, & Skip-Tracing**
PFF   **Bail-Bond & Bounty-Hunting for Fugitives**
PFG   **Martial Arts & Self-Defense** (including Armed & Unarmed Hand-to-Hand
                   Combat, Personal Weaponry, Marksmanship, & Swordsmanship)
                   NOTE: Class Combat Sports at KJK. Class Gunsmithing & Bladesmithing at MHC.
PFH   **Bodyguards & Protection**
PFN   **Polygraph**
PFO   **Other Topics Related to Police Science**

PG   **Criminal Justice, Penology, Parole, Corrections, & Rehabilitation**

PH   **Military Science**
PHA   **Study & Teaching of Military Science** (including War College, ROTC Programs,
                   Basic Training, Military Schools & Academies, Maneuvers, War Games, & Military
                   Museums)
PHB   **Military History**
PHC   **Military Traditions, Protocol, Uniforms, Medals, & Insignia**
PHD   **Command Structure & Organization of Armies**

PHE	Theory & Philosophy of Warfare (including Strategy & Tactics)
	EXAMPLE: *The Art of War* by Sun-tzu
PHF	Military Facilities, Hardware, Vehicles, Ordnance, Weapons, & Delivery Systems
	NOTE: Class Gunsmithing & Bladesmithing at MHC.
PHG	Infantry
PHH	Cavalry (including Air Cavalry & Armored Cavalry)
PHI	Artillery
PHJ	Special Commando Units
PHK	Military Engineering, Construction, & Demolition
PHL	Military & Strategic Intelligence (also, Espionage & Counter-espionage)
PHLA	Terrorism & Counter-terrorism
PHM	Military Logistics
PHN	Military Communication
PHO	**Military Aviation** (including Air Power, Military Air Transport, Air Support, Air & Space Warfare, Air Force, & Space Force)
PHP	Military Law & Military Justice (including *Uniform Code of Military Justice*, Judge Advocate General's Corps, Military Police, Military Prisons, & Courts Martial)
PHQ	Prisoners of War
PHR	Martial Law & Military Administration
PHS	Other Topics Related to Military Science (including Combat Medics & Military Hospitals)

PI	**Naval Science**
PIA	Study & Teaching of Naval Science (including Naval Academies, Naval ROTC, Naval Maneuvers, & Boot Camp)
PIB	Naval History
PIC	Naval Traditions, Protocol, Uniforms, & Insignia
PID	Command Structure & Organization of Navies
PIE	Theory & Philosophy of Naval Science (including Naval Tactics)
PIF	Naval Facilities, Hardware, Vehicles, Vessels, & Weapons
PIG	Fleet Operations
PIH	Seamanship
PII	Navigation
PIJ	Naval Artillery
PIK	Submarine Operations
PIL	SEALs & Naval Commandos
PIM	Naval Engineering, Construction Battalion, & Naval Architecture
PIN	Naval Intelligence
PIO	Naval Logistics
PIP	Naval Discipline & Justice (including Shore Patrol , NCIS, & Brigs)
PIQ	Naval Air Power
PIR	Coast Guard
PIS	Marine Corps
PIT	Other Topics Related to Naval Science (including Naval Medical Corps)

Q   Behavioral Sciences

QA   **Cultural Anthropology**
QAA   Periodicals & Yearbooks Devoted to Cultural Anthropology
QAB   Study & Teaching of Cultural Anthropology (including Fellowships &
        Scholarships, Schools, Tutorials, & Museums of Cultural Anthropology)
QAC   History of the Discipline of Cultural Anthropology (including Biographies
        of noted Anthropologists, such as Margaret Mead)
QAD   Theory & Philosophy of Cultural Anthropology (including Methodology)
QAE   Geographic Treatment of Cultural Anthropology
        NOTE: Here must be classed actual works of Cultural Anthropology (studies of human
        societies & cultures around the world).
QAEA   Europe & Islands of the Atlantic Ocean
QAEB   Africa
QAEC   Middle East
QAED   South Asia
 QAEE   Islands of the Indian Ocean
QAEF   Far East (including Southeast Asia & Malaysia)
QAEG   Australia & New Zealand
QAEH   Islands of the Pacific Ocean
QAEI   North America
QAEJ   Central America & Islands of Caribbean
QAEK   South America

QB   **Sociology**
QBA   Periodicals & Yearbooks Devoted to Sociology
QBB   Matters of Practical, Ethical, or Legal Concern to Persons Working
        in Fields Related to Sociology
        EXAMPLE: Licensing of Social Workers & Counselors
QBC   Study & Teaching of Sociology (including Fellowships & Scholarships, Degree
        Programs, Tutorials in Sociology)
QBD   Geographical & Historical Treatment of Sociology
QBE   Socialization
QBF   Social Stratification
QBG   Comparative Sociology (Comparison of Social Processes Between Nation States
        or Across Different Types of Society, such as Capitalist & Socialist)
QBH   Sociology of Specific Groups within Society
QBHA   Women
QBHB   Men
QBHC   Teens
QBHD   Children
QBHE   Ethnic Groups & Immigrant Communities
QBI   Rural & Small-Town Sociology
QBJ   Suburban Sociology
QBK   Urban Sociology

QBL	Criminology & Differential Sociology (including Triads, Mafia, Criminal Gangs, & Demimonde)
QBM	Mores
QBN	Fads, Trends, & Pop Culture
	NOTE: Class Social Movements & Influences here.
QBO	Social Change (including Social Evolution, Social Revolution, & Future Society)
QBP	Phenomenon of Celebrity
QBQ	Customs & Institutions
QBQA	Courtship Rituals, Marriage Customs, & Sexual Practices
QBQB	Funereal Customs
QBR	Counterculture, Alternative Lifestyles, & Non-conformity (including Sociological Studies of Polyamory, LGBT, Single Lifestyle)
QBS	Utopian Experiments
QBT	Social Workers, Counselors, & the Work They Do (including Social Services & Child Protective Services)

QC   **Psychology**

NOTE: Class Clinical Psychology at RRI & Forensic Psychology at RRID.

QCA	Dictionaries & Encyclopedias of Psychology
QCB	Study & Teaching of Psychology (including Fellowships & Scholarships, Schools, & Seminars)
QCBA	Experimental Psychology
QCC	Geographical & Historical Treatment of Psychology
QCD	Theories of Psychology
QCE	Popular Psychology
QCF	Physiological Psychology
QCFA	Phrenology
QCG	States of Consciousness (including Subconscious, Hypnotic State, Sleep, Dreams, & Symbols)
	NOTE: Class Hypnosis as a Therapeutic Tool at RRI.
QCH	Cognitive & Perceptual Psychology (including Learning, IQ, Creativity, & Memory)
QCI	Differential Psychology (including Character & Personality)
QCJ	Male Psychology
QCK	Female Psychology
QCL	Developmental Psychology (including Psychology of Children & Teenagers)
QCM	Social Psychology
QCN	Psychology of Ethnic Groups & Other Groups
QCO	Environmental Psychology
QCP	Industrial & Organizational Psychology
QCQ	Comparative or Animal Psychology
QCR	Parapsychology

R   **Health Sciences**

RA   Dictionaries & Encyclopedias Related to Health Sciences

RB   Associations Devoted to Health Sciences

RC   Periodicals & Yearbooks Devoted to Health Sciences

RD   Matters of Practical, Ethical, or Legal Concern to Persons Working in Fields Related to Health Sciences

EXAMPLES: Licensing of Physicians & Nurses, Ethics of Euthanasia, & Malpractice Liability

RE   Related Arts & Science to Health Sciences

RF   Study & Teaching of Health Sciences (including Fellowships & Scholarships, Schools, Training Seminars, & Museums of Health Sciences)

RG   Geographical & Historical Treatment of Health Sciences

RH   Theory & Philosophy of Health Sciences

RI   Medical Equipment & Nursing Supplies

RJ   **Public Health & Safety**

RJA   Fire Safety & Firefighting

RJB   Ambulance & Rescue Service

RJC   Medicare, Medicaid, & Health Insurance

RJD   Centers for Disease Control, Departments of Health, World Health Organization, etc

RJE   Epidemiology

RK   **First Aid**

RL   Nursing Care & the Nursing Profession (including RNs, Practical Nurses or LVNs, Physicians' Assistants, & Nursing-Care Facilities)

RM   **Medical Care & the Medical Profession**

RMA   General Practice (including Internal Medicine & Family Practice)

RMB   Medical Specialization

RMC   Pediatrics

RMD   Geriatrics, Longevity, & Life Expectancy

RME   New & Evolving Specialties (including Environmental, Aerospace, & Sports Medicine)

RMF   Functional or Holistic Medicine

RN   Preventive Medicine (including Vaccinations)

RO   Self-Care & Healthy Lifestyle (including Exercise & Yoga for Physical Health)

RP   Palliative Care & Hospice Care

RP   **Hospitals & Clinics**

RPA   ERs & Emergency Care

RPB   Field Hospitals

RPC   Triage

RQ   **Human Anatomy & Physiology**

RQA   Human Reproductive Process

RQB   Obstetrics & Gynecology

RQBA   Childbirth (including Midwifery)

RQBB   Neonatal Care

RQC   Nutrition (including Diets & Dieting)

RQD   Gastroenterology

RQE	Nephrology
RQF	Urology
RQG	Endocrinology
RQH	Hematology
RQI	Rheumatology
RQJ	Cardiology
RQK	Pulmunology (Respiratory Medicine)
RQL	Neurology
RQM	Podiatry
RQN	Dermatology
RQO	Ophthalmology, Optometry, & Optical Dispensing
RQP	Hearing Loss & its Correction
RR	**Diseases & Disorders**
RRA	Pathology, Etymology, & Progression of Diseases
RRAA	Forensic Pathology
RRB	Symptomatology
RRC	Trauma
RRD	Toxicology
RRE	Communicable Diseases
RREA	Zoonoses
RRF	Birth Defects
RRG	Oncology
RRH	Immunology
	NOTE: Class Allergies here.
RRI	**Psychiatry & Clinical Psychology** (including Disorders, Conditions, & Treatments not specifically mentioned below)
	NOTE: Class *Diagnostic & Statistical Manual of Mental Disorders* here. Class General Psychology at QC.
RRIA	Dependency & its Treatment (including AA & RR, Alcoholism, & Eating Disorders)
RRIB	Affective Disorders (Mood Disorders, including Bi-Polar Disorder & Depression)
RRIC	Self-Help Psychology
	NOTE: Class here Meditation & Yoga for Mental Health, Self-Hypnosis, & Stress Management.
RRID	Forensic Psychology
RS	**Medical Diagnostics**
RSA	Radiology, Diagnostic Imaging, CAT Scans, & MRIs
RT	**Treatment & Therapeutics** (including Pain Management, Physical Therapy, Bariatrics, & Therapeutic Massage)
RTA	Nuclear Medicine
RU	Surgery
RUA	Anesthesiology & Anesthetics
RV	**Alternative Medicine**

RVA	Homeopathy
RVB	Chiropractics
RVC	Reflexology (including Acupuncture & Acupressure)
RVD	Folk Remedies & Home Remedies
RVE	Herbalism
RW	**Pharmaceutical Science**
RX	**Mortuary Science**

S   **Nature's Bounty**

SA   Environmentalism & Conservation

SAA   Renewable Energy

SB   Forestry & Land Management

SC   Wildlife Management

SCA   Animal Control

SCB   Pest Control

SD   Wilderness Skills & Survival

SDA   Foods & Medicines from the Wild

           NOTE: Class Foraging here.

SE   **Commercial Hunting & Trapping**

           NOTE: Class Trophy Hunting & Hunting for Sport at KO.

SF   Commercial Fishing

           NOTE: Class Fishing as a Pastime or Sport at KO.

SG   **Prospecting & Drilling**

           NOTE: Class Dowsing here; also, Treasure Hunting.

SH   Mining & Exrtraction

T		**Agricultural Science**
TA		Dictionaries & Encyclopedias Related to Agricultural Science
TB		Associations Devoted to Agricultural Science (including 4-H Clubs & Future Farmers of America or FFA.)
TC		Periodicals & Yearbooks Devoted to Agricultural Science
TD		Matters of Practical, Ethical, or Legal Concern to Persons Working in Fields Related to Agricultural Science
TE		Related Arts & Science to Agricultural Science
		EXAMPLE: Farm Economics
TF		Study & Teaching of Agricultural Science (including Fellowships, Scholarships, & Schools)
TFA		County Agents
TG		Geographical & Historical Treatment of Agricultural Science
TH		Theory & Philosophy of Agricultural Science
TI		Equipment, Tools, & Supplies Related to Agricultural Science
TJ		Soil Science
		NOTE: Class Crop Rotation & Fallowing here.

TK		**Horticulture**
TKA		Orchards & Tree Farming
TKB		Field Crops
TKC		Herb & Vegetable Gardening
TKD		Greenhouse Gardening
TKE		Hydroponics
TKF		Mushroom Cultivation
TKG		Ornamental Horticulture
		NOTE: Class Floriculture here. Class Floristry at LGG.

TL		**Animal Husbandry**
TLA		Pets
TLAA		Animal Shelters
TLB		Working Animals
TLC		Livestock
TLCA		Bovine Stock
TLCB		Equine Stock
TLCC		Sheep & Goats
TLCD		Small Stock
TLCE		Exotic Stock
TLD		Apiary (Beekeeping & Honey Production)
TLE		Aquaculture (including Fisheries)

U   Veterinary Medicine

V	History & Related Arts & Sciences
VA	Associations Devoted to History
VB	Periodicals & Yearbooks Devoted to History
VC	Study & Teaching of History (including Fellowships & Scholarships, Schools, Tutorials, & History Museums)
VD	Historical Research & Historiography
VE	Art of Biography
VEA	Miscellaneous Biographies, Autobiographies, Memoirs, & Diaries
VF	Archaeology
VG	Comprehensive History of the World
VGA	Prehistory
VGB	Ancient Times
VGC	The Middle Ages 476 CE – 1453 CE
VGD	The Renaissance 1453 CE – 1700 CE
VGE	18th Century
VGF	19th Century
VGG	20th Century
VGH	21st Century
VH	Histories of the Various Peoples & Regions of the World
VHA	Europe & Islands of the Atlantic
VHAA	Prehistoric Europe
VHAB	Ancient Europe
VHAC	The Middle Ages 476 CE – 1453 CE
VHAD	The Renaissance 1453 CE – 1700 CE
VHAE	18th Century
VHAF	19th Century
VHAG	20th Century
VHAH	21st Century
VHB	Africa
VHC	The Middle East
VHD	South Asia & Islands of the Indian Ocean
VHE	Far East (including Southeast Asia & Malaysia)
VHF	Australia, New Zealand, & the Pacific Islands
VHG	The New World (Western Hemisphere)
VHH	North America
VHHA	Pre-Columbian Civilizations
VHHB	1492 CE – 1700 CE
VHHC	18th Century
VHHD	19th Century
VHHE	20th Century
VHHF	21st Century
VHI	Central America & Islands of the Caribbean
VHJ	South America
VI	Comprehensive Histories of Specific Groups

VIA	Women
VIB	Blacks
VIC	Hispanics
VID	Indigenous Peoples
VID	Histories of Other Groups

W	Geography & Exploration

W   **Geography & Exploration**

WA   Associations Devoted to Geography & Exploration
          EXAMPLE: National Geographic Society

WB   Periodicals & Yearbooks Devoted to Geography, Exploration, & Travel
          EXAMPLE: *Journal of the National Geographic Society*

WC   Study & Teaching of Geography

WD   Historical Geography

WE   Cartography (including Surveying)

WEA   Maps, Atlases, & Gazetteers

WF   **Travel & Tourism**

WFA   Clubs & Associations Devoted to Travel & Tourism

WFB   Travel Agents & Agencies

WFC   Matters of Practical, Ethical, or Legal Concern to Tourists, Tour Guides, & Travel Agents (including Passport & Visa Requirements)

WG   **Regional Geography** (including Travel & Tourism within Specific Regions)

WGA   Europe & Islands of the Atlantic

WGB   Africa

WGC   Middle East

WGD   South Asia & Islands of the Indian Ocean

WGE   Far East (including Southeast Asia & Malaysia)

WGF   Australia, New Zealand, & Pacific Islands

WGG   New World (Western Hemisphere)

WGGA   North America

WGGB   Central America & Islands of the Caribbean

WGGC   South America

WGH   Arctic & Antarctica

WGI   Destinations Defined by some Commonality of Features
          EXAMPLES: Islands, Cities, Tropics, Mountains, etc.

X	Transportation
XA	Primitive or Non-motorized Transportation
XB	**Automotive Transportation** (including Driving Skills)
XBA	Associations Devoted to Automotive Transportation
XBB	Periodicals & Yearbooks Devoted to Automotive Transportation
XBC	Automotive Vehicles & Trailers (including Motorcycles, Scooters, & Electric Vehicles, & Trucks)
XBD	Automotive Sales & Rentals
XBE	Vehicle Maintenance & Repair
XBEA	Body Shop & Collision Repair
XBF	Equipment, Tools, & Supplies Related to Automotive Transportation
XBG	Driver Training & Licensing
XBH	Rules of the Road (including *Driver's Handbooks*)
XBI	Highway Systems & Roadways
XC	**Public Transportation**
XD	Comprehensive Works on Freight Transport
XE	**Rail Transportation**
XF	**Maritime Transportation**
XFA	Ships & Boats of the High Seas & Inland Waterways
XFB	Merchant Marine or Merchant Navy in the UK (including Mariners, Uniforms, Traditions, & Protocol)
XFBA	Merchant Marine Academies
XFBB	Commercial Shipping (including Ocean Liners & Freighters)
XFC	Maintenance & Repair of Ships & Boats
XFD	Sailing
XFE	Knots & Knot-tying
XFF	Maritime Navigation (including Dead Reckoning, Celestial Navigation, & Mariners' Ephemerides)
XFG	Maritime Charts
XFH	Maritime Safety (including Boating Regulations & Convention on the High Seas)
XFI	Maritime Signals & Communication
XFJ	Chandlers & Chandlery
XG	**Air Transportation**
XGA	Airports, Terminals, & Ground Facilities
XGB	Air-Traffic Control
XGC	Aircraft & Lighter-Than-Air Craft
XGCA	Aircraft Maintenance
XGD	Aviation
XGDA	Remote Control of Aircraft
	NOTE: Class Drones here.
XGDB	Gliding, Jet-packing, etc
	NOTE: Class Aerial Sports at KJI.
XGE	Parachuting
XGF	Air Safety

XGG	Flight Navigation
XGH	Flight Communication
XGI	Flight Control
XGJ	Air Passenger Service
XGK	Air Freight Service
XH	**Space Travel**

NOTE: Class here Space Agencies, Astronauts & Cosmonauts, NASA, the Space Race, & *The Right Stuff,* Rocketry, Space Ships, Commercial Space Travel, Space Stations & Artificial Satellites, Rovers & Extraterrestrial Vehicles, Lunar Landers, Space Shuttles, Space Suits, & other Equipment. Class UFOs & Extraterrestrial Lifeforms at NVL.

INDEX

18th Century

Art of the World IGE

English-Language Literature GHD

English-Language Poetry GRHD

European History VHAΞ

European Art IGIE

History of North America VHHC

History of the World VGE

Literature of the World GGE

North American Art IGOC

Poetry of the World GRGD

19th Century

Art of the World IGF

English-Language Literature GHE

English-Language Poetry GRHE

European Art IGIF

History of Europe VHAF

History of North America VHHD

Histry of the World VGF

Literature of the World GGF

North American Art IGOD

Poetry of the World GRGE

20th Century

Art of the World IGG

English-Language Literature GHF

English-Language Poetry GRHF

European Art IGIG

History of Europe VHAG

History of North America VHHE

History of the World VGG

Literature of the World GGG

North American Art IGOE

Poetry of the World GRGF

21st Century

Art of the World IGH

English-Language Literature GHG

English-Language Poetry GRHG

European Art IGIH

History of Europe VHAH

History of North America VHHF

History of the World VGH

Literature of the World GGH

Poetry of the World GPGG

North American Art IGOF

4-H Clubs TB

Abacus   NLCA
Abbreviations, Standard   DF
Abstract Art, Non-objective   IKH
Absurdist Drama   HSF
Academies   PA
     Merchant-Marine   XFBA
     Military   PHA
     Naval   PIA
     Police   PFA
Accessories, Fashion (Manufacturing of)   OJL
Accounting   PC
Acoustical Engineering   OIL
Acquisitions (Library Science)   CAH
Acrostics (Poetry)   GREF
Acrylic Medium for Modeling   MD
Acrylic Painting   INAA
Acting   HM
     Screen   HVM
Acupuncture & Acupressure   RVC
Adaptation (Script Writing for Motion Pictures)   HVK
Adding Machines   NLCA
Administration
     Business   PC
     Church   BM
     Military   PHR
     School   PA
Adobe Construction   MAJC
Advanced Mathematics   NLG
Advertising   PC
Aerial Sports   KJI
Aerospace Engineering   OII
Aerospace Medicine   RME
Aesthetics   BYJ
Affective Disorders   RRIB
Africa
     Art History   IGJ
     Cultural Anthropology   QAEB
     Geography, Travel, & Exploration   WGB
     History   VHB
Agents & Agencies, Travel   WFB
Agricultural Architecture & Construction   MAO
Agricultural Engineering   OIO
Agricultural Science   T
Agricultural Tools, Equipment, & Machinery (Manufacturing of)   OJH
Air Cavalry   PHH
Air Force   PHO
Air Power   PHO

Visual   I
Asceticism   BNC
Assemblage (Art)   ING
Asset Management   PC
Assistance, Research (Library Science)   CAKA
Associations   AE
    Devoted to Agricultural Science   TB
    Devoted to Architecture & Construction   MAB
    Devoted to Automotive Transportation   XBA
    Devoted to Dramatic Arts   HB
    Devoted to Geography & Exploration   WA
    Devoted to Health Sciences   RB
    Devoted to History   VA
    Devoted to Language Arts & Communication   DB
    Devoted to Leisure, Hobbies, Sports, & Recreation   KB
    Devoted to Library Science   CAA
    Devoted to Literature & its Creation   GB
    Devoted to Motion-Picture Arts & Sciences   HVB
    Devoted to Music   JB
    Devoted to Photography   INJB
    Devoted to Poetry   GRB
    Devoted to Science   NB
    Devoted to Technology, Engineering, & Manufacturing   OB
    Devoted to Travel, Exploration, & Tourism   WFA
    Devoted to Visual Art   IB
Astrobiology   NVL
Astrochemistry   NVI
Astrogeology   NVK
Astrology   NVA
Astrometry   NVJ
Astronauts   XH
Astronomy   NV
Astrophysics   NVH
Atlantic Islands
    Art History   IGI
    Geography, Travel, & Exploration   WGA
    History   VHA
    Cultural Anthropology   QAEA
Atlases   WEA
Audio Recording (Information Storage)   CD
Aum Shinrikyo   BI
Australia
    Cultural Anthropology   QAEG
    Geography & Exploration   WGF
    History   VHF
    Art History   IGM
Autobiographies   VEA

Automotive Engineering   OIN
Automotive Transportation   XB
Automotive Vehicles, Manufacturing of   OJI
Available-Light Photography   INJL
Aviation   XGD
      Military   PHO
      Naval   PIQ
Avionics   OIJ
Awards for
      Dramatic Arts   HD
      Literature   GF
      Motion Pictures   HVD
      Music   JD
      Photography   INJD
      Poetry   GRF
      Sports   KD
Axiology   BYH
Badges, Police   PFC
Bahá'í Faith   BHE
Bail-Bond   PFF
Ballads (Poetry)   GREA
Ballet   JVD
Ballroom Dancing   JVB
Bandstands   MASB
Bangladeshi Art   IGK
Barbering   LBA
Bariatrics   RT
Bar-Mitzvah Photography   INJO
Barns (Architecture & Construction)   MAO
Bartending   LGE
Basic Training, Military   PHA
Basketry   MI
Beads, Beading, & Beadwork   MGA
Beauty Contests & Titles   LBB
Beekeeping   TLE
Behavioral Sciences   Q
Beliefs of Humanity   B
Beliefs, False   BA
Belly Dance   JVF
Benediction   BNB
Beverage Service   LGE
Bible, Christian & Commentaries   BEA
Bindery   GPC
Binomial Nomenclature   NSA
Biographies   VEA
      of Cultural Anthropologists   QAC
      of Individuals Associated with Multiple Areas of the Arts   EB

Buddhism   BGC
Burlesque   HX
Business Arts   PC
Cabinetry   MAKK
CAD-CAM   OEB
Calculators   NLCA
Calculus   NLG
Calendars   NVE
Calligraphy   DG
Camping   KO
Candle-making   MJ
Car Clubs   XBA
Card Games   KKB
Cardiology   RQJ
Caribbean Islands
  Art History   IGN
  Cultural Anthropology   QAEJ
  Geography, Travel, & Exploration   WGGB
  History   VHI
Carnivals   KQ
Carpentry, Construction   MAJA
Cartography   WE
Cartooning   INC
Cartoons (Recreation & Relaxation)   KM
Casinos   KKF
CAT Scans   RSA
Cataloging (Library Science)   CAJ
Catalogs of Art Exhibitions   IFA
Catering   LGEA
Catholic Church, Roman   BECC
Cattle Ranching & Farming   TLCA
Cavalry   PHH
CDC   RJD
Ceilings   MAKH
Celebration of Life   BN
Celebrity, Phenomenon of   QBP
Celestial Navigation   XFF
Censorship, Motion-Picture   HVD
Centers for Disease Control   RJD
Central America
  Art History   IGO
  Cultural Anthropology   QAEJ
  Geography, Travel, & Exploration   WGGB
  History   VHI
Ceramics   MD
Chandlers & Chandlery   XFJ
Change, Social   QBO

Character   QCI
Charcoal Drawing   INB
Charts, Maritime   XFG
Chemical Engineering   OIP
Chemicals, Manufacturing of   OJJ
Chemistry   NU
Child Protective Services   QBT
Childbirth   RQBA
Child-rearing   LDA
Children
     Artworks by   IM
     Psychology of   QCL
     Sociology of   QBHD
Chiropractics   RVB
Choreography   JVC
Christianity   BE
Chronometry   MF
Cinematography   HVR
Cinquain   GREI
Circuses   HW
Citizenship   PD
City Planning   MASC
Cityscapes (Art)   IKF
Civics   PD
Civil Engineering   OIE
Civil-Rights Movement   PDA
Civil Rights   PD
Civil Service   PD
Classical Music   JP
Classical Philosophy   BYA
Classification
     of All Living Things   NSA
     Library   CAI
Clerihews   GREF
Climate   NRA
Climbing   KO
Clinical Psychology   RRI
Clinics   RP
Clip Art   II
Clock-Making   MF
Cloisonne   MGB
Cloud Storage   CCC
Clowns   HW
Clubs (Also see Associations.)
     Devoted to Travel, Exploration, & Tourism   WFA
     Astronomy   NVB
     Car   XBA

Fan (for Movies & Movie Stars)   HVB
Coast Guard   PIR
Cob Construction   MAJI
Coding   CCBA
Cognitive Psychology   QCH
Collage   INH
Collected Literary Works & Criticisms   GG
Collecting
    Art   IH
    as a Hobby   KNA
    Photographic Art   INJG
Collections, Special (Library Science)   CAHA
Collision Repair   XBEA
Color (Studio Art)   IJC
Combat Medics   PHS
Combat Sports   KJK
Combat, Armed & Unarmed Hand-to-Hand (Self-Defense)   PFG
Combinatronics   NLB
Comedies, Motion-Picture   HVXF
Comedy
    Dramatic Arts   HSB
    Stand-up   HX
Comic Books   GOJ
Command Structure
    of Armies   PHD
    of Navies   PID
Commandos   PHJ
    Naval   PIL
Commercial Hunting, Fishing, & Trapping   SE
Commercial Architecture & Construction   MAN
Commercial Art   IJE
Commercial Photography   INJM
Commercial Shipping (Maritime)   XFBB
Communicable Diseases   RRE
Communication   D
    Flight XGH
    Maritime   XFI
    Military   PHN
    Business   PC
Communities
    of the Arts   EB
    Utopian   QBS
Comparative Philosophy   BY
Comparative Psychology   QCQ
Comparative Religion   BB
Comparative Sociology   QBG
Composition

Artistic   IJB
Literary   GPA
Musical   JJ
Photographic   INJJ

Comprehension, Reading for   DGA
Computational Mathematics   NLG
Computer Engineering   OIH
Computer Games   KKE
Computer Science   CC
Computer-Assisted Design   OEB
Computerized Information Storage & Retrieval   CCC
Computerized Systems (Construction Electrical Trade)   MAKB
Computers, Manufacturing of   OJF
Concerts   JMA
Concrete Construction   MAJD
Conducting Music   JMD
Confucianism   BGE
Congregations, Christian   BEC
Consciousness, States of   QCG
Conservation   SA
Conservatories, Music   JF
Constellations   NVD
Construction & Architecture   MA
Construction Battalion, Navy   PIM
Construction Materials, Manufacturing of   OJM
Construction Trades   MAK
Construction, Military   PHK
Consumer & Industrial Electronics, Manufacturing of   OJF
Contests
    Beauty   LBB
    Photography   INJD
Control
    Air-Traffic   XGB
    Animal   SCA
    Flight   XGI
    Pest   SCB
    Remote   OIJ
        of Aircraft   XGDA
Convention on the High Seas   XFL
Cookery   LGD
Coptic Christianity   BECA
Copyright
    Art   ID
    Law   PE
    Literature   GPA
    Music   JD
Corrections (Criminal Justice)   PG

Cosmetology   LBA
Cosmology
          Philosophical   BYF
          Scientific   NVM
Cosmonauts   XH
Costumes
          Motion-Picture   HVQ
          Theatrical   HQ
Counseling   QBT
          Pastoral   BL
Counselors   QBT
Counterculture   QBR
Counter-espionage   PHL
Counter-Reformation, The   BEBC
Counter-terrorism   PHLA
Counting   NLB
Country & Western Music   JTD
County Agents   TFA
Coup d'état   PD
Courts Martial   PHP
Courtship   QBQA
Crafts   M
Crayon Drawing   INB
Creative Writing   GPA
Creativity   QCH
Crime Stories   GOF
Criminal Justice   PG
Criminology   QBL
Criticisms, Collected Literary   GG
Crocheting   MKC
Crop Rotation   TJ
Cross Stitch   MKD
Cruise Ships   KP
Cryptology & Cryptography   DN
Cult Religions   BI
Cultural Anthropology   QA
Culture (The Arts)   E
Curiosities   AG
Customs   QBQ
Cutting with a Torch   MHD
Cybernetic Engineering   OIJ
Damnation   BK
Dance   JV
Darkroom   INJK
Dead Reckoning at Sea   XFF
Deafness   RQP
Decorating with Flowers   LGG

Decorating, Interior   MASA
Decoration, Table   LGH
Decoupage   INH
Deists   BJ
Deities   BK
Delivery Systems (Ordnance)   PHF
Demimonde   QBL
Demolition   MAL
Demolition, Military   PHK
Demonology   BK
Dendrology   NSGD
Denominations
        Christian   BEC
        Protestant   BECE
Departments of Health   RJD
Dependency & its Treatment   RRIA
Depression
        Affective Disorder   RRIB
        The Great
                History of North American   VHHE
                History of the World   VGG
Depth of Field (Photography)   INJJ
Dermatology   RQN
Design
        Factory   OIT
        Floral   LGG
        Interior   MASA
        Stage Sets   HP
        Studio Art   IJD
Destructive Testing   OIB
Detective Stories   GOF
Determinism   BYI
Developing, Photographic   INJK
Development, Software   CCBA
Developmental Psychology   QCL
Diagnostics (Clinical Psychology)   RRI
Diaries of Literary Figures   GG
Diction   DI
Dictionaries   DA
        of Agricultural Science   TA
        of Architecture & Construction   MAA
        of Dramatic Arts   HA
        of Health Sciences   RA
        of Leisure, Hobbies, Sports, & Recreation   KA
        of Literature   GA
        of Motion-Picture Arts & Sciences   HVA
        of Music   JA

of Photography INJA
of Poetry GRA
of Psychology QCA
of Science NA
of Technology, Engineering, & Manufacturing OA
of Visual Art IA
Polyglot DAA
Diets & Dieting RQC
Differential Psychology QCI
Differential Sociology QBL
Digital Editing HVS
Dining LGF
Diplomacy PD
Directing
      Motion-Picture Arts & Sciences HVN
      Stagecraft HN
Discrete Mathematics NLG
Diseases RR
Dish-washing LF
Disorders RR
Dispensing
      Optical RQO
      Pharmaceutical RW
Distribution PC
Diving KJJ
Dizain GREI
Docudramas HVXC
Documentary Films HVXB
Dolls KS
Domestic Relationships LD
Doors MAKJ
Dowsing SG
Drafting OEA
Dramatic Arts H
Drawing INB
      Mechanical OEA
Dreams QCG
Drilling (Prospecting) SG
Driving (Automotive Transportation) XB
Drones (Air Craft) XGDA
Druidism BC
Druze Faith BHA
Dry Cleaning LC
Drywall Construction MAKF
DVDs of Motion Pictures HVY
Early Church (Historical Christianity) BEBC
Earth Science NO

Earthquakes   NPB
Earth-sheltered Construction   MAJG
Eastern Orthodoxy   BECB
Eating Disorders   RRIA
Ecclesiastical Architecture & Construction   MAQ
Ecclesiastical Music   JQ
Ecclesiology   BM
Ecology   NSI
Economics   PB
Economics   PB
     Farm   TE
     Home   LE
Ecosystems   NSI
Editing
     Books & the Printed Word   GPB
     Photographic Images   HVS
Education   PA
Education, Driver   XGB
Efficiency Engineering   OIV
Eighteenth Century   See 18th Century.
Ekphrases   GREC
Elections   PD
Electric Vehicles   XBC
Electrical Engineering   OIG
Electrical Trade, Construction   MAKA
Electronic Engineering   OIG
Electronic Games   KKD
Electronics, Consumer & Industrial (Manufacturing of)   OJF
Elegies   GREC
Elves   BV
eMail   DS
Embellishment, Architectural   MAT
Emergency Care   RPB
Emergency Service   RJB
Enameling   MGB
Encaustic   INAG
Encyclopedias   AA
     of Agricultural Science   TA
     of Architecture & Construction   MAA
     of Dramatic Arts   HA
     of Health Sciences   RA
     of Leisure, Hobbies, Sports, & Recreation   KA
     of Literature   GA
     of Motion-Picture Arts & Sciences   HVA
     of Music   JA
     of Photography   INJA
     of Poetry   GRA

Related to Photography   INJI
Related to Police Science   PFC
Related to Scientifiuc Inquiry   NI
Related to Sports & Recreation   KI
Ergonomics   OIU
Erotic Art   IKC
Erotic Literature   GOE
Erotic Photography   INJS
Erotic Verse   GRED
ERs   RPA
ESL, Study & Teaching of   DDA
Espionage   PHL
Etching   IND
Ethics   BYI
     Medical   RD
Ethnic Groups
     Psychology of   QCN
     Sociology of   QBHE
Etiquette   LA
Etymology
     of Disease   RRA
     of Words   DF
Europe
     Art History   IGI
     Cultural Anthropology   QAEA
     Geography, Travel, & Exploration   WGA
     History   VHA
Euthanasia   RD
Event Photography   INJO
Events, Sporting   KJ
Evolution
     of the Universe   NVM
     Social   QBO
     Theory of   NS
Exercise (Self-Care & Healthy Lifestyle)   RD
Exhibition of Motion Pictures   HVT
Exhibitions, Art   IFA
Existentialism   BYCA
Exotic Dance   JVF
Exotic Livestock   TLCE
Experimental Mathematics   NLG
Experimental Psychology   QCBA
Exploration   W
Exposure (Photography)   INJJ
Exrtraction of Minerals   SH
External Hard Drives   CCC
Extra-Sensory Perception   QCQ

Extraterrestrial Life   NVL
Extraterrestrial Vehicles   XH
Facial Expressions   DK
Facilities for Sports & Recreation   KI
Facilities
        Military   PHF
        Naval   PIF
Factory Design   OIT
Factory Operation   OJ
Fads   QBN
Fairies   BV
Fairs   KQ
Faith   BR
Faith-Healing   BR
Fallowing   TJ
Family Medical Practice   RMA
Fan Clubs for Movies & Movie Stars   HVB
Fanfares   JO
Fantasy Literature   GOH
Far East
        Art History   IGL
        Cultural Anthropology   QAEF
        Geography, Travel, & Exploration   WGE
        History   VHE
Farm Machinery
        Agricultural Engineering   OIO
        Agricultural Science   TI
Fashion Photography   INJM
Fashions   LBD
Fate   BYI
Feedback   OIJ
Fellowships
        in Agricultural Science   TF
        in Architecture & Construction   MAF
        in Cultural Anthropology   QAB
        in Dramatic Arts   HF
        in Health Sciences   RF
        in History   VC
        in Language Arts & Communications   DD
        in Library Science   CAD
        in Literature   GD
        in Motion-Picture Arts & Sciences   HVF
        in Music   JF
        in Photography   INJF
        in Poetry   GRD
        in Psychology   QCB
        in Science   NF

in Sociology	QBC	
in Visual Art	IF	
Female Artists	IGQA	
Female Authors & their Works		GNA
Female Poets & their Works	GRNA	
Female Psychology	QCK	
Feminism	PDA	
Ferns (Botany)	NSGB	
FFA	TB	
Fiction	F	
Field Crops	TKB	
Field Hospitals	RPB	
Figure photography	INJS	
Film Editing	HVS	
Film Schools	HVF	
Finance, Household	LE	
Financial Management		PC
Fine Art	I	
Fire Safety & Firefighting		RJA
First Aid	RK	
Fish (Ichthyology)	MSHF	
Fisheries	TLE	
Fishing		
Commercial	SF	
Sports	KO	
Flags, Signal	DN	
Flash Drives	CCC	
Fleet Operations	PIG	
Flight, Science of	XGD	
Floors	MAKI	
Floppy Discs	CCC	
Floriculture	TKG	
Floristry	LGG	
Flowering Plants (Botany)		NSGC
Flowers, Language of	DJ	
Focus (Photography)	INJJ	
Folk Art	IM	
Folk Dancing	JVA	
Folk Literature		GGA
Folk Music	JS	
Folk Remedies	RVD	
Food Products, Manufacturing of		OJA
Food Service	LGE	
Foods from the Wild	SDA	
Foraging	SDA	
Foreign Languages, Study & Teaching of		DDB
Forensic Pathology	RRAA	

Forensic Psychology   RRID
Forestry   SB
Formal Science   NK
Fortunetelling   BS
Framing
    Art   IFB
    Construction Carpentry   MAJA
    Photography   INJK
Free Will   BYI
Fraternal Orders   AE
Freethinkers   BJ
Freight Service, Air   XGK
Freight Transport   XD
Freighters (Maritime Commercian Shipping)   XFBB
French-Language Literature   GI
French-Language Poetry   GRI
Fresco Technique   INAH
Friends of the Library   CAC
Friendship   LD
Functional Medicine   RMF
Funereal Customs   QBQB
Fungi   NSD
Furniture Design & Construction   MC
Furniture, Library   CAF
Future Farmers of America   TB
Future Society   QBO
Future Technologies   OL
Gambling   KKF
Game Theory   NLG
Games   KK
    Manufacturing of   OJC
    War   PHA
Gaming   KKF
Gangs, Criminal   QBL
Gardens, Botanical   NSGA
Garments, Manufacturing of   OJL
Gastroenterology   RQD
Gazebos   MASB
Gazetteers   WEA
Gemology   NPDA
Gems, Language of   DJ
General Medical Practice   RMA
General Works   A
Genre Art   IKE
Geographic Treatment of Cultural Anthropology   QAE
Geography   W
Geology   NP

Geometry   NLE
Geriatrics   RMD
German Literature   GJ
German-Language Poetry   GRJ
Ghazal   GREI
Ghosts   BU
Glamour Photography   INJS
Glass Craft   ME
Glass Work in Construction   MAJF
Gliding (Aviation)   XGDB
Gnomes   BV
Goats   TLCC
God(s)   BK
Golden Shovels   GREF
Goldsmithing   MHA
Gouache   INAF
Government   PD
Grammar   DF
Graphic Novels   GOJ
Greek Orthodox Church   BECB
Greenhouse Gardening   TKD
Grooming & Personal Appearance   LB
Ground Facilities (Air Transportation)   XGA
Gryphons   BV
Guidance Systems   OIJ
Gunsmithing   MHC
Gymnastic   KJF
Gynecology   RQB
Haiku   GREI
Halls of Fame, Sports   KG
Hardware
        Computer   CCA
        Military   PHF
        Naval   PIF
Hats, Manufacturing of   OJL
Hauntings   BU
Healing through Faith   BR
Health Sciences   R
Hearing Loss & its Correction   RQP
Heating   MAKD
Heaven   BK
Hebrew Scriptures & Commentaries   BDA
Hell   BK
Hematology   RQH
Herb Gardens   TKC
Herbalism   RVE
Herpetology   NSHC

Hierarchy, Clerical   BM
Highways   XBI
Hiking   KO
Hinduism   BGB
Hip-Hop   JTB
Hispanic Artists   IGQC
Hispanic Authors & their Works   GNC
Hispanic Poets & their Works   GRNC
Hispanics, Comprehensive Histories of   VIC
Historical Christianity   BEB
Historical Drama   HSF
Historical Fiction   GOG
Historical Geology   NPA
Historical Islam   BFB
Historical Judaism   BDB
Historiography   VD
History   V
     of Agricultural Science   TG
     of Architecture & Construction   MAG
     of Arts in General   EB
     of Cultural Anthropology   QAC
     of Dramatic Arts   HG
     of Exploration & of Tourism   WD
     of Health Sciences   RG
     of Law Enforcement   PFB
     of Leisure, Hobbies, Games, Sports, & Recreation   KG
     of Library Science   CAE
     of Literature   GG
     of Motion-Picture Entertainment   HVG
     of Music   JG
     of Navies, Naval Science, & Naval Warfare   PIB
     of Philosophy   BY
     of Photography   INJH
     of Poetry   GRG
     of Psychology   QCC
     of Science   NG
     of Sociology   QBD
     of Technology   OG
     of the World   VG
     of Visual Art   IG
     of Warfare & Military Science   PHB
Holiness   BK
Holistic Medicine   RMF
Holy Bible & Commentaries   BEA
Holy Family (Historical Christianity)   BEBA
Holy Quran & Commentaries   BFA
Holy Writ (Comprehensive & Comparative Works)   BQ

Home Arts   L
Home Improvement   MAL
Home Remedies   RVD
Homeopathy   RVA
Homiletic   BP
Honey Production   TLE
Horology   MF
Horror Films   HVXE
Horror Stories   GOI
Horse Ranching   TLCB
Horticulture   TK
Hospice Care   RP
Hospitality   LG
Hospitals   RP
     Military   PHS
Hourglasses   MF
Household Finance   LE
Household Goods & Appliances, Manufacturing of   OJD
Housekeeping   LF
Hula Dance   JVF
Human Figure (Art Theme)   IKC
Human Resources   PC
Humanism   BYCA
Humor (Recreation & Relaxation)   KM
Humor, Literary   GOD
Hunting, Commercail   SE
Hunting, Trophy   KO
Hydroponics   TKE
Hymns
     Use in Worship   BO
     Music   JQ
Hypnosis
     Therapeutic Tool   RRI
     Self-   RRIC
Hypnotic State   QCG
Ichthyology   MSHF
Iconographic Art   IKA
Illumination   INC
Illustration   INC
Imaging, Diagnostic   RSA
Immigrant Communities, Sociology of   QBHE
Immunology   RRH
Impasto   INAD
India & Indian-Ocean Islands
     Art History   IGK
     Cultural Anthropology QAEE
     Geography, Travel, & Exploration   WGD

History   VHD
Indigenous Artists & their Works   IGQD
Indigenous Authors & their Works   GND
Indigenous Peoples, Comprehensive Histories of   VID
Indigenous Poets & their Works   GRND
Individual Sports   KJD
Industrial Architecture & Construction   MAR
Industrial Engineering   OIT
Industrial Photography   INJN
Industrial Production   OJ
Industrial Psychology   QCP
Industrial Revolution
      European History   VHAF
      History of Technology   OG
      World History   VGF
Industry, Broadcast   HU
Infantry   PHG
Influences, Social   QBN
Information Science   C
Inn-keeping   LGB
Innovative Construction Methods & Materials   MAJI
Insects (Invertebrate Zoology)   NSHI
Insignia
      Military   PHC
      Naval   PIC
Inspirational Literature (Philosophy & Religion)   BX
Institutional Architecture & Construction   MAP
Institutions (Sociology)   QBQ
Instructional Films   HVXB
Instrumentation   OIJ
Instruments, Musical   JI
Insurance
      as Related to Public Health & Safety   RJC
      Medical-Malpractice   RD
Integrated Electronic Systems (Construction Electrical Trade)   MAKB
Intelligence Quotient   QCH
Intelligence
      Military & Strategic   PHL
      Naval   PIN
Interior Design   MASA
Internal Medicine   RMA
Internet   DR
Intrigues, Literary   GOF
Invertebrates   NSHI
Investigation (Police Science)   PF
Ironing/Pressing   LC
Islam   BF

Jainism   BHD
Jazz   JTA
        Dance   JVE
Jesus & the Holy Family   BEBA
Jet-packing   XGDB
Jewelry   MG
Jokes   KM
Journaling   KNC
Journalism   GQ
Journals, Literary   GC
Judaism   BD
Judge Advocate General's Corps   PHP
Judgment, Final   BK
Jugglers   HW
Jurisprudence   PE
Justice
        Military   PHP
        Naval   PIP
Juvenile Literature   GOA
Juvenile Verse   GREH
Kismet   BYI
Knitting   MKC
Knots & Knot-tying   XFE
Knowledge (Epistemology)   BYG
Knowledge, General   A
Laboratories, Science   NI
Labour Churches   BJ
Land Management   SB
Landscape Architecture   MASB
Landscape Art   IKF
Landscape Photography   INJT
Language Arts   D
Lapidary   MG
Lasar Technology   OIM
Latter Day Saints   BECF
Laundry   LC
Law   PE
        Martial   PHR
        Military   PHP
Leadership
        Busines Arts   PC
        Political Science   PD
Learning
        Cognitive & Perceptual Psychology   QCH
        Education   PA
Leasing, Automotive   XBD
Leisure   K

LGBT Community (Sociology)   QBR
Library Science   CA
Licensed Vocational Nurses   RL
Licensing
        Architecture & Construction   MAD
        Engineering, Technology & Manufactiring   OD
        Drivers   XBG
Life Science   NS
Light Verse   GREF
Lighter-Than-Air Craft   XGCA
Lighting
        Motion-Picture Arts & Sciences   HVO
        Photography   INJJ
        Stagecraft   HO
Lighting Equipment, Manufacturing of OJE
Lightroom®   INJK
Limericks   GREF
Linocut   IND
Literary Fiction   GOC
Literature   G
Lithography   IND
Livestock   TLC
Lobbyists   PD
Location Photography   INJL
Logic   BYD
Logistics
        Military   PHM
        Naval   PIO
Longevity   RMD
Looms   MKA
Lorries   XBC
Love Poems   GRED
Love Stories   GOE
Lumber Processing   OJM
Lunar Astronomy   NVF
Lunar Rovers   XH
LVNs   RL
Lyrical Poetry   GREC
Lyrics to Songs   JL
Machinery
        Art Theme   IKGA
        Farm (Agricultural Engineering)   OIO
        Manufacturing of   OJG
Machining   MHE
Mafia   QBL
Magic   BT
Maintenance

of Aircraft
of Automotive-Vehicle XBE
of Buildings   MAL
of Ships & Boats   XFC
Malaysia
  Art History   IGL
  Cultural Anthropology   QAEF
  Geography, Trave, & Exploration   WGE
  History   VHE
Male Psychology   QCJ
Malpractice, Medical   RD
Mammalogy   MSHG
Management
  Business Arts   PC
  Engineering   OIC
  Hotel   LGB
  Land   SB
  Library   CAG
  Pain   RT
  Restaurant   LGC
  Stress   RRIC
  Theater   HR
  Wildlife   SC
Maneuvers
  Military   PHA
  Naval   PIA
Manichaeism   BHB
Manipulation, Photo   INJK
Manufacturing   OJ
Maps   WEA
Marine Corps   PIS
Marine Vessels, Manufacturing of   OJI
Maritime Navigation   XFF
Maritime Sports   KJJ
Maritime Transportation   XF
Marketing   PC
Marketing   PC
Marksmanship   PFG
Marksmanship Sports   KJL
Marriage Customs   QBQA
Martial Arts   PFG
Martial Law   PHR
Martial Music   JR
MASH Units   PHS
Masonry Construction   MAJB
Massage
  Erotic   QBQA

             Therapeutic   RT
Materialism   BYCA
Materials
          Construction Methods   MAJ
          Construction Supplies   MAI
          Engineering   OIA
Mathematical Logic   NLG
Mathematics   NL
Measurements, Standardization of   PD
Mechanical Drawing   OEA
Mechanical Engineering   OID
Mechatronics   OIJ
Medals, Military   PHC
Media, Art   IN
Medicaid   RJC
Medical Care & the Medical Profession   RM
Medical Corps, Naval   PIT
Medical Photography   INJN
Medicare   RJC
Medicine, Veterinary   U
Medicines from the Wild   SDA
Medics, Combat   PHS
Medieval Literature
          English-Language   GHB
                    Poetry   GRHB
          of the World   GGC
                    Poetry   GRGB
Medieval Philosophy   BYB
Meditation
          Religious Practice   BNC
          Self-help Psychology   RRIC
Melodrama   HSD
Memoirs   VEA
Memory   QCH
Men, Sociology of   QBHB
Merchant Marine (Merchant Navy in the UK)   XFB
Mermaids   BV
Metalcraft   MH
Metaphysics   BYE
Meteorology   NR
Method, Scientific   NH
Methodology in Cultural Anthropology   QAD
Methods, Construction   MAJ
Microbiology   NSC
Microfiche Records   CB
Microfilm Records (Library Science)   CB
Microscopy   NSCA

Middle Ages
  European Art History IGIC
  European History VHAC
  World Art History IGC
  World History VGC
Middle East
  Geography, Travel, & Exploration WGC
  Art History IGK
  Cultural Anthropology QAEC
  History VHC
Midwifery RQBA
Military Science PH
Mimes HW
Mineralogy NPD
Miniaturization OIK
Mining SH
Miracles BT
Mixed-Media Art INH
Mixology LGE
Model-Building for Architects MAE
Modeling Clay MD
Modeling, Mathematical NLG
Models
  Building & Collecting as a Hobby KNB
  Fashion and Glamour LBC
Modern Dance JVE
Modern Philosophy BYC
Modern Rabbinical System BDD
Modular Construction MAJH
Monera NSF
Monographs, General Collected A
Montage INH
Montage, Photo INJW
Mood Disorders RRIB
Mood in Photography INJJ
Moral Philosophy BYI
Morality Plays HSF
Mores QBM
Mortuary Science RX
Mosaic INE
Mosses (Botany) NSGB
Motion Pictures HVY
Motion-Picture Arts & Sciences HV
Motion-Picture Themes JO
Motor Sports KJH
Motorcycles XBC
Mounting Photographic Prints INJK

Movements
      Islamic BFC
      Social QBN
MRIs   RSA
Murals   INAH
Museography, Art   IFA
Museology, Art   IFB
Museums   PA
      of Cultural Anthropology   QAB
      of Curiosities & Oddities   AG
      of Health Sciences   RF
      of History   VC
      of Literature   GD
      of Military History   PHA
      of Motion-Picture Arts & Sciences   HVF
      of Photography   INJF
      of Science   NF
      of Visual Art   IFA
Mushroom Cultivation   TKF
Music   J
Musical Drama   HSE
Musicals, Motion-Picture   HVXG
Mysteries
      General Works   AD
      Literary Theme   GOF
      Motion-Picture Theme   HVXH
Mythology   BCA
Nail Salons   LBA
Nanotechnology   OIK
Narrative Verse   GREA
NASA   XH
Native Americans   See Indigenous Peoples.
Native Crafts   MM
Natural History   NN
Natural Religion   BJ
Natural Science   NM
Naturalism (Art Appreciation)   IH
Nature Art   IKF
Nature's Bounty   S
Naval Science   PI
Navigation
      Flight   XGG
      Maritime   XFF
      Naval Science   PII
NCIS   PIP
Needlepoint   MKD
Negotiation (Business Arts)   PC

Neighborhood Watches   PFD
Neon Signs   DH
Neonatal Care   RQBB
Nephrology   RQE
Netsuke   MM
Neurology   RQL
New Age Music   JTE
New World
     Geography, Travel, & Exploration   WGG
     History   VHG
New Zealand
     Cultural Anthropology   QAEG
     Geography, Travel, & Exploration   WGF
     History   VHF
     Visual Art   IGM
Night Photography   INJL
Nineteenth Century   See 19th Century.
Non-conformity (Sociology)   QBR
Non-destructive Testing   OIB
Non-fiction   GOB
Non-flowering Plants (Botony)   NSGB
Non-motorized Transportation   XA
Non-objective Art   IKH
Non-theistic Churches   BJ
North America
     Art History   IG**O**
     Cultural Anthropology   QAEI
     Geography, Travel, & Exploration   WGGA
     History   VHH
Notation
     Dance   JVC
     Music   JK
Nuclear Engineering   OIS
Nuclear Medicine   RTA
Nude Art   IKC
Nude Photography   INJS
Numbers   NLA
Nursing Care   RL
Nutrition   RQC
Nutritional Supplements, Manufacturing of   OJA
Nymphs   BV
Obeah   BC
Observatories   NVC
Obstetrics   RQB
Occult Arts   BW
Ocean Liners   XFBB
Oceanography   NQ

Octopi (Invertebrate Zoology)   NSHI
Oddities   AG
Odes   GREC
Office Skills   PC
Oil Painting   INAA
Oncology   RRG
Ontology   BYFA
Oology   MSHE
Operatic Music   JO
Operating Systems, Computer   CCBB
Operation
          Factory   OJ
          Fleet   PIG
          Submarine   PIK
Ophiomancy   BS
Ophthalmology   RQO
Optical Dispensing   RQO
Optical Engineering   OIM
Optometry   RQO
Oral Traditions (Religion & Ancient Systems of Belief)   BCA
Oratory   DI
Orchards   TKA
Ordnance   PHF
Organization
          of Armies   PHD
          of Churches   BM
          of Libraries   CAI
          of Navies   PID
Organizational Psychology   QCP
Oriental Art
          Far Eastern   IGL
          Near Eastern & South Asian   IGK
Oriental Religion & Philosophy   BG
Ornamental Horticulture   TKG
Ornithology   MSHD
Orthodoxy, Eastern   BECB
Orthography   DF
Pacific Islands
          Art History   IGM
          Cultural Anthropology   QAEH
          Geography, Travel, & Exploration   WGF
          History   VHF
Packaging   OK
Paganism   BC
Pageantry   HV
Pain Management   RT
Painting

Construction Trades MKAG
Studio Art INA
Paints, Manufacturing of OJJ
Paleogeology NPA
Paleontology NSB
Palindromes (Poetry) GREF
Palliative Care RP
Palmistry BS
Papacy BECD
Papier Mâché MD
Parachuting XGE
Paradelle GREI
Parades HV
Parapsychology QCR
Parenting LDA
Parks
　　　Landscape Architecture MASB
　　　Amusement KQ
　　　Wilderness KOA
　　　Zoological NSHA
Parole (Criminal Justice) PG
Parties, Political PD
Parts, Automotive XBF
Party Planning LGA
Passenger Service, Air XGJ
Passports WFC
Pastels (Art Medium & Technique) INB
Pastoral Theology BL
Pastoral Verse GREB
Pathology RRA
Pathways MASB
Patrol (Police Science) PF
Pediatrics RMC
Pen-&-ink INB
Pencil Drawing & Sketching INB
Penmanship DG
Penology PG
Perceptual Psychology QCH
Performance, Musical JM
Period Fiction GOG
Periodicals AC
　　Devoted to Photography INJC
　　Devoted to Agricultural Science TC
　　Devoted to Architecture & Construction MAC
　　Devoted to Automotive Transportation XBB
　　Devoted to Cultural Anthropology QAA
　　Devoted to Dramatic Arts HC

Post-Production, Motion-Picture   HVS
Pottery   MD
Practical Nurses   RL
Prayer   BNB
Pre-Columbian Art   IGOA
Pre-Columbian Civilizations of North America   VHHA
Prefabricated Construction Methods   MAJH
Prehistoric Art
          of Europe   IGIA
          of the World   IGA
Prehistoric Europe   VHAA
Prehistoric Systems of Belief   BC
Prehistory   VGA
Preservation of Artworks   IFB
Preventive Medicine   RN
Primitive Art   IM
Primitive Transportation   XA
Printed Word   GP
Printing, Photographic   INJK
Printmaking   IND
Prisoners of War   PHQ
Prisons   PG
          Military   PHP
Private Security & Investigations   PFE
Prizes
          for Literature   GF
          for Poetry   GRF
Production Management   PC
Production Notes (Stagecraft)   HT
Production
          on an Industrial Scale   OJ
          Motion-Picture   HVL
          Stage   HL
Professional Photography   INJJ
Prognostication, Weather   NRBA
Program Music   JN
Promotion
          Business Arts   PC
          of Motion-Picture   HVU
          of Stage Plays   HR
Pronunciation   DI
Proofreading   GPB
Prophesy   BS
Prophet Muhammad   BFB
Props
          Motion-Picture   HVQ
          Theatrical   HQ

Recreation   K
Recycling (Sanitation Engineering)   OIF
Reflexology   RVC
Reformation, The   BEBD
Regional Geography   WG
Registered Nurses   RL
Regulations
     Boating   XFH
     Related to Architecture & Construction   MAD
     Related to Engineering, Technology & Manufactiring   OD
Rehabilitation, Criminal   PG
Reincarnation   BK
Relaxation   K
Release of Motion Pictures   HVT
Religion & Philosophy   B
Religion   BB
Religious Art   IKB
Remote Control   OIJ
     of Aircraft   XGDA
Renaissance
     English-Language Literature   GHC
     English-Language Poetry   GRHC
     European Art   IGID
     European History   VHAD
     Literature of the World   GGD
     Poetry of the World   GRGC
     World History   VGD
Rendering, Architectural   MAE
Renewable Energy   SAA
Renovation   MAL
Rentals, Automobile   XBD
Repair
     of Automotive Vehicle   XBE
     of Books   CAH
     of Ships & Boats   XFC
Reproductive Process, Human   RQA
Reptiles   NSHC
Rescue Service   RJB
Research
     Historical   VD
     Library   CAKA
Residential Architecture & Construction   MAM
Resorts   KP
Respiratory Medicine   RQK
Restaurants   LGC
Restoration, Art   IFB
Retouching, Photographic   INJK

Revelation BS
Revenants BU
Reviews
of Motion Pictures HVY
of Plays HT
Revolution, Social QBO
Rheumatology RQI
Rhythm-&-Blues JTB
Riddles KL
Rides, Amusement KQ
Rites (Worship) BNA
Rituals
Courtship QBQA
Religious BNA
RNs RL
Roadways XBI
Robotics OIJ
Rock-&-Roll JTC
Rocketry XH
Roman Catholicism BECC
Romantic Love Stories GOE
Romantic Relationships LD
Romanticism (Art Appreciation) IH
Rom-Coms, Motion-Picture HVX⁼
Rondel GREI
Roofs MAKH
ROTC PHA
Naval PIA
Rules of Order PC
Rules of the Road XBH
Rural Sociology QBI
Russian Orthodox Church BECB
Russian-Language Literature GK
Russian-Language Poetry GRK
Sacraments BNA
Sacred Music
Musical Treatment JQ
Use in Worship BO
Safety RJ
Flight XGF
Maritime XFH
Sailing XFD
Saints, Christian BEBB
Sales PC
Automotive XBD
Salvation BK
Sanitation Engineering OIF

Scrying BS
Sculpture INF
SD Cards CCC
Seabees PIM
SEALs & SEAL Teams PIL
Seamanship PIH
Seances BU
Seasons of the Year NVE
Secret Societies AE
Sects
       Christian BEC
       Islamic BFC
       Jewish BDC
Security Systems, Building MAKC
Seismology NPB
Self-Care & Healthy Lifestyle RO
Self-Defense PFG
Self-Flagellation BNC
Self-Help Psychology RRIC
Self-Hypnosis RRIC
Semaphore Communication DM
Seminars in Psychology QCB
Serigraphy IND
Sermons BP
Service Industries PC
Services, Photographic INJI
Sestina GREI
Set Design
       Motion-Picture Arts & Sciences HVP
       Stage Craft HP
Set Theory NLG
Sewing MKB
Sex (Human Reproductive Process) RQA
Sexual Practices QBQA
Sexual Relationships LD
Sheds, Decks MASB
Sheep TLCC
Sheet Music JU
Sheet-Metal Fabrication MHF
Shelters, Animal TLAA
Shintoism BGA
Shipbuilding OJI
Ships XFA
       Cruise KP
Shoes, Manufacturing of OJL
Shore Patrol PIP
Short Films HVXA

Shorthand   PC
Shrubs (Dendrology)   NSGD
Signal Flags   DN
Signals, Maritime   XFI
Signing & Sign Languages   DL
Signs & Sign-Lettering   DH
Sikhism   BHF
Silk Screen   IND
Silos (Architecture & Construction)   MAO
Silversmithing   MHA
Sin   BK
Singing   JMA
Single Lifestyle   QBR
Sketching   INB
Skip-Tracing   PFE
Sleep   QCG
Slide Rule   NLCA
Small-Stock Husbandry   TLCD
Small-Town Sociology   QBI
SMS   DR
Snails (Invertebrate Zoology)   NSHI
Snake-Handling (Religion)   BR
Snap-shooting   INJW
Social Media   DR
Social Philosophy   BYK
Social Psychology   QCM
Social Sciences   P
Social Services   QBT
Social Workers   QBT
Socialization   QBE
Sociology   QB
Software   CCB
Soil Science   TJ
Solar Astronomy   NVE
Soldering   MHD
Sonnets   GREE
Sorcery   BT
Soul Music   JTB
South America
          Art History   IGP
          Cultural Anthropology   QAEK
          Geography & Exploration   WGGC
          History   VHJ
South Asia
          Art History   IGK
          Cultural Anthropology   QAED
          Geography, Travel, & Exploration   WGD

	History	VHD
Southeast		
	Art History	IGL
	Cultural Anthropology	QAEF
	Geography, Travel, & Exploration	WGE
	History	VHE

Space Force   PHO
Space Travel   XH
Space Warfare   PHO
Spanish-Language Literature   GL
Spanish-Language Poetry   GRL
Special Collections (Library Science)   CAHA
Special Effects, Motion-Picture   HVV
Specialization, Medical   RMB
Spectroscopy   NVJ
Speech   DI
Spelling   DF
Spiders (Invertebrate Zoology)   NSHI
Spirits (Ghosts)   BU
Spiritualism   BU
Sports Equipment, Manufacturing of   OJC
Sports Fishing   KO
Sports Medicine   RME
Sports Photography   INJP
Sports   KJ
Spy Novels   GOF
Square Dancing   JVA
Squids (Invertebrate Zoology)   NSHI
Stables (Architecture & Construction)   MAO
Stage Production   HL
Stairs   MAKI
Standardization of Weights & Measurements   PD
Stand-up Comedy   HX
Statesmanship   PD
Statistics   NLG
Statistics, Sports   KG
Steel Construction   MAJE
Still Life
        Art   IKG
        Photography   INJV
Stone-cutting   ML
Stone-Engraving   DH
Strategy, Military   PHE
Stratification, Social   QBF
Straw-Bale Construction   MAJI
Street Photography   INJR
Stress Management   RRIC

Strip Tease   HX
Structural Engineering   OIE
Studio Art   IJ
Studio Photography   INJJ
Study

      of Agricultural Science   TF
      of Architecture & Construction   MAF
      of Arts in General   EA
      of Botany   NSGA
      of Cultural Anthropology   QAB
      of Dramatic Arts   HF
      of English as a Foreign Language   DDA
      of Foreign Languages   DDB
      of Geography   WC
      of Health Sciences   RF
      of History   VC
      of Language Arts & Communications   DD
      of Library Science   CAD
      of Literature   GD
      of Military Science   PHA
      of Motion-Picture Arts & Sciences   HVF
      of Music   JF
      of Naval Science   PIA
      of Photography   INJF
      of Physical Education, Sports, & Recreation   KF
      of Poetry   GRD
      of Police Science   PFA
      of Psychology   QCB
      of Science   NF
      of Sociology   QBC
      of Technology, Engineering, & Manufacturing   OF
      of Zoology   NSHA
Stunts (Motion-Picture Arts & Sciences)   HVV
Style Manuals   DF
Style, Individual Artistic   IJG
Subconscious Mind   QCG
Submarine Operations   PIK
Suburban Sociology   QBJ
Summer Sports   KJB
Sundials   MF
Sunrise & Sunset   NVE
Superlatives   AF
Superstitions   BA
Supplies

      Agricultural   TI
      Art   II
      Automotive Repair & Transportation   XBF

on Sociology	QBC		
on Visual Art	IF		

Twentieth Century   See 20th Century.

Twnety-first Century   See 21st Century.

Typing   PC

UFOs   NVL

Unconventional Construction Methods & Materials   MAJI

Undercover Police Operations   PF

Unicorns   BV

Unification Church   BI

Uniforms

    Merchant-Marine   XFB

    Military   PHC

    Naval   PIC

    Police   PFC

    School   PA

Upholstery   MCA

Urban Sociology   QBK

Urology   RQF

User Services (Library Science)   CAK

Utopian Experiments   QBS

Vaccination   RN

Value & Valuation (Axiology)   BYH

Vampires   BV

Vaudeville   HX

Vegetable Gardening   TKC

Vehicles

    as a Theme in Art   IKGA

    Automotive   XBC

    Manufacturing of   OJI

    Military   PHF

    Navy   PIF

    Police   PFC

Vehicular Engineering   OIN

Ventilation   MAKD

Vertebrates   NSHB

Vessels, Naval   PIF

Vestments, Clerical   BM

Veterinary Medicine   U

Vibrations (Acoustical Engineering)   OIL

Vice (Moral Philosophy)   BYI

Video Recording (Information Storage & Retrieval)   CD

Vigilantes   PFD

Villanelle   GREI

Virtue   BYI

Visa Requirements   WFC

Visual Art   I

Voice & Singing   JMB
Volcanoes   NPC
Voodoo   BC
Vulcanology   NPC
War College   PHA
War Games   PHA
          Naval   PIA
Wardrobe Maintenance   LC
Waste Management   OIF
Watch-Making   MF
Water Features   MASB
Water Purification & Distribution   OIF
Watercolor   INAE
Wattle Construction   MAJI
Weapons
          Military   PHF
          Naval   PIF
          Personal   PFG
          Police   PFC
Weather   NRB
Weaving   MKA
Wedding Photography   INJO
Weights & Measurements, Standardization of   PD
Welding   MHD
Werewolves   BV
Western Hemisphere
          Geography, Travel, & Exploration   WGG
          Art History   IGN
          History   VHG
Western World, Art of the   IGI
Westerns
          Literary Theme   GOGA
          Motion-Picture Theme   HVXD
WHO   RJD
Wilderness Parks   KOA
Wilderness Recreation   KO
Wilderness Survival   SD
Wildlife Art   IKDA
Wildlife Management   SC
Windows (Architecture & Construction)   MAKJ
Winter Sports   KJA
Wireless Communication   DQ
Wisdom   BX
Witchcraft   BT
Women
          Comprehensive Histories of   VIA
          Poets & their Works   GRNA